LOVE'S WHISPERINGS

Authentic Spiritual Development

LOVE'S WHISPERINGS

Authentic Spiritual Development

Chireya

Part 1: Source Awakening Series
Including transmissions from the
Star Elders of the Council of Human Enlightenment
Star Elders of the Council of Mu
Divine Mother & Divine Father
With Introduction by Sanat Kumara

FOXY CREATIONS WORLDWIDE

LOVE'S WHISPERINGS
Authentic Spiritual Development
Book One: Source Awakening Series

By Chireya

© Copyright 2015 by Laura C. Fox and
Foxy Creations Worldwide, LLC, All Rights Reserved.

No portion of this material may be duplicated in any form without express written permission of the author, with the exception of short quotes to be used to share wisdom and information about these writings.

LOVESWHISPERINGS.COM
CHIREYA.COM

ISBN 978-0-9907498-0-6

Dedication

*This book is dedicated to YOU
in your awakening
and to the Source of All Life,
called by many names ~
God, Love, Jesus, Allah, Buddha,
Tao, Source, All That Is,
Life, Love, True Self,
Ever Present Origin,
Omnipresent Being,
Prime Creator,
The One*

GRATITUDE

*Special thanks to
Tom Bird, Mixtress Hava, Rama Jon,
Master K, Greg, Humphrey, Gwen Payne,
Ben, Zach, Eric & Denise, Brittney Turnpaugh,
Sonya Sophia, Jennifer Partridge, Debra Giusti,
Brad Nye, Keith Michael Virgo, Marcelo Hamui,
Andrea & Peter Post, Dan & Pete Cruger,
Carol Fitzpatrick, Carole Dore,
Larisa Stow, Michael Perlin,
and many others for
holding space in
so many ways
seen and
unseen.*

*I love and appreciate
you all.*

It's All Here For You

*Open and aspire to the highest and best vibration
you are able to embody in this lifetime.
It is all here for you.*

*The gateways are open, the time is now, and you
are an important part of the Cosmic Awakening at
hand. Thank everyone in your life, even those
beings who have caused you pain. Thank life itself,
your mother planet and all beings and experiences
for bringing
you to where you are now.*

*Be At One with the knowing that your life
is unfolding perfectly as planned.*

*Become willing to realize that all that has come
before was the result of the actions, feelings,
thoughts and words that came before them.*

*The zero point is nearly here.
The great rebalancing is in progress.*

*You are a Divine Being, and you are here
to serve through your own divine gifts in the
grand unfoldment of human potential.*

~ *The Star Elders*

Contents

Prologue	15
The Field of All Creative Potential	20
Chireya: Early Training & Intention	22
Tune In	25
Opening Message	29
Love's True Power	33
The Profound Nature of Awakening	41
Your Cosmic Calling Card	49
EXERCISE: *Accessing the Love Within You for Guidance*	49
EXERCISE: *Accessing Your Cosmic Calling Card*	54
Support for Your Vibration	63
EXERCISE: *Complete Clearing of Component 1*	70
Restoring Foundational Support for *Your Vibration in Component 1*	72
Support for Your Vibration in Component 2	77
Affirmations for Supporting *Your Vibration In Component 3*	83
Support for Your Vibration In Component 4	88
Support for Your Vibration In Component 5: Your Historical Context	95
Support for Your Vibration In Component 6	101
The Pink Light of Unconditional Love	104
Core Star Activation	105

Actions To Accelerate Healing	*105*
7 Affirmations for Returning To Truth	*106*
Listening To The Inner Voice: Starseed Technologies	109
Tools of the Deception	123
What does love do? What does fear do?	*125*
Correcting Spiritual Misperceptions	131
The Three Divine Precepts	*133*
Technique for Overcoming Projection When Experiencing An Emotional Charge	*144*
EXERCISE: Source Alignment Process	*146*
An Alternative View On A Second Coming	157
Living In Divine Principle	163
The Five Divine Principles	*167*
Simplify Life	*172*
EXERCISE: Align with Flow & Simplicity	*175*
Closing Message	183
Chireya's Tips for Recalibrating Your Life	191
The Master Key To Liberation	*194*
Action Steps for Recalibrating Your Life	*195*
Appendix I. Resources	199
Appendix II. Glossary	203
Chireya	211

SAY YES TO LOVE

*When you say so, the battle is over.
You say so by being the love that you are.
This love encompasses all, embraces all, forgives all, sees all, knows all and loves all.
You 'be' this love by simply allowing.
Simply allow the love that you are to flow radiantly from within the core of your being to all around you. Say yes to love and love says yes to you.
Love will show you how. This is the end of all duality, this is the end of all suffering, and this is the release from all bondage.
This sheds new light on the words,
'love your enemies.'
Why would one love ones enemies unless that love would cause the release from enmity?
And so it does, so it will.*

~ *The Star Elders of the Council of Human Enlightenment**

PROLOGUE

*There is no battle, there is only the
shining radiance of Pure Divine Love's True Power*

In the vast, wild and largely unknown history of the planet, Star Beings have interacted with human beings, for better and for worse. Many are the channels, scientific discoveries and translations of ancient texts that explain our history is far more interesting that we have supposed.

Also hidden have been the codes of comprehension of who we are and how the universe works. The purpose of this book is not to indulge in the nitty gritty details of this history, but instead to reveal a system of knowledge and wisdom that can help us comprehend the base operating system of reality, so we can relate to it more intentionally, and discard outworn beliefs and patterns like dirty old clothes. Yes, we will be getting naked to a set of truths which can indeed set us free.

The core of the message has to do with our original, untouchable divinity. Regardless of "how" our physical bodies were created, the ultimate truth is, the Primordial Presence of Life Itself is what animates, informs and lives through these bodies.

The Prime Creator, God, has indeed initiated all of Creation, and from this Original Spark, "we" have all emerged as aspects of the One.

As our Spirit became Soul and embarked on a journey through time and space, these bodies were formed. The genetic lineages of the bodies, the lifetimes of the Soul and the conditioning in this life combine to create through us patterns of thought and feeling sometimes called our "vibrational offering." This vibrational offering flies out into the ethers of life capturing bits of energy that are similar in quality, and flinging these energy bits into our lives like a cosmic boomerang. These energy bits show up as "experiences" in life. Because of our lack of training and comprehension of these things, we are often caught unawares and wonder, "why me?"

Compounding this, intentional deception from beings who sought control and manipulation as their prime motivation in relating with the rest of humanity further veiled the truth of who we are and how we operate as cosmic beings, aspects of the Prime Creator in form. This veiling complicated matters to a degree where divine intervention has been deemed necessary to 'get the cosmic wedgie' out of humanity's tale so that it can more fully get on with the business of aspiring to its own self-realization.

Even though these beings calling themselves God may have monkeyed around or tinkered with people, places and things causing cascading cycles of separation and suffering, this Prime Creator ALWAYS exists in all, as all, through all. For this Great Law of One cannot be overridden. It is a fact. As we awaken to this realization, we can indeed begin to embody the truths and practices presented here. This Spirit In Us is the spirit of Love — a true love that is ever present, always whispering to our souls, our minds, our bodies, reminding us to come 'home' to the truth of this love, and to spread it's glory wherever we go.

And as we realize this "fact" of the Law, we will also realize that to push against, make wrong or judge ANY other being, would only further compound our own sticky vibrational wicket. Therefore, we get support in this book for the comprehension necessary to truly and fully forgive everything and everyone, for everything that could possibly need to be forgiven.

The Star Elders, First Mother & First Father explain that without understanding the base software program of reality which says, "that which goes around comes around," it is extremely challenging and perhaps impossible to fully embrace these Universal Laws.

When this basic comprehension fully lands in a being, as much as half of the energetic backlog of blockage within an individual may be eliminated quickly if not immediately. People experience tremendous relief, simply from comprehending on a core level, why things are they way they are and how we got here. Then, the person can focus upon calibrating to the new, creative vision and Divine Plan for their lives, which is truly co-creative.

When the time ripens for a person to fully express themselves here in the earth plane and manifest their gifts to the world, the experiences of this embodied spirit blends with the particular gifts cultivated as soul through many incarnations.

Source has shown me that the Divine Plan for the whole and the individual, is not static. It is more like a base platform with certain key codes that get activated through the life experience of a being (over many lifetimes). The nature of the "codes" endowed within the being by the Prime Creator allow for deep reflection and the design of a life plan based on relevance, joy and a desire to contribute to the whole.

The person can then bring forth their unique codes into this world as a co-created gift. This co-creation develops from attunement with the original divine blueprint (the cake) plus the mastery, experiences and inspirational life achievements by the person (the icing) towards the goal of relevant sharing of one's Aspect with All of Creation, to move it forward.

My gift that I have cultivated to be "relevant" at this time of awakening, is in helping people "recalibrate" to the divine energies of their authentic life path. The Recalibration Process™ is a fourfold process: Attune, Align, Dissolve, Design. The experience of recalibration helps people attune to their Divine Blueprint (the pattern), align directly with Source within (the power), dissolve energetic residue and barriers to success (the problems), and design their life based on their latest upgraded divine destiny path (the icing on the cake).

We are at a time on earth where the revelation of our true essence and gifts is the hallmark of the day. Who are you? What is your purpose? How did you get here? How can you serve, here and now, with joy, fulfillment, clarity, knowing and more fun than humans have formerly been allowed to have? Indeed, how can you prosper and thrive, shedding the rusty mechanics of a world gone awry, fully embracing the new possibilities of co-creation through a unified field of love?

The Field of All Creative Potential

The love that you are fulfills all need. Be still and know that you are God. Embrace the God and Love that you are entirely, wholly, fully, and completely so that there is nothing else but you, God and this love. From this place of complete surrender, you will be restored, you will be blessed and you will know what to do in your earthly life to make it as beautiful and powerful and loving as it can possibly be.

Know that all is well as you lift yourself out of the vibrations of the past and deliver yourself into the arms of your Creator. From this place of connection, the inspiration will flow to assist you in fulfilling your particular mission and role in life's unfolding drama. There is no other, there is only One, so everywhere you look, you look upon the face of God, the One, as an expression of love. The collective ceremony of separation has created innumerable belief systems currently in need of dissolution. Truth and forgiveness will replace misunderstanding and pain as we open ourselves to receive these divine teachings.
~ The Star Elders

When "being" with these Ancient Ones and Masters of the Lineages of Light on the inner planes and in sessions, the experience is that of a "We." I am aware of myself as an individuated aspect of Self, while simultaneously aware of the Collective. "We" are all immersed in and held by a beautiful, expansive, eternal "Field". In this state, the human mind is whole instead of dual. "We" are all in total harmony, aware of ourselves as one and individuated simultaneously "in The Field." The Field of All Creative Potential is where we "sit" and "reside."

Human beings can learn to enter this Field with one another for any purpose desired. This Field is beyond and inclusive of the Collective, which one may call the All That Is, God, Source, or Pure Love. In it is a deeper peace than many experience in a lifetime, and all possibilities exist here. It is from here that I see, feel and know that we can collectively solve our human and earthly problems, attain spiritual liberation, and enjoy true Divine Communion in a Direct Source experience.

A Direct Source experience occurs when we are aware that divinity is within us, just as Masters such as Jesus and Buddha have taught. For example, Jesus' (Yeshua's) legacy to the world includes the sanction, "Be still, and know that ye are God." Jesus also beckons us to "Seek ye first the Kingdom of God, and all else shall be added unto you." And where is this Kingdom? "The Kingdom of God is within You." And Buddha chose to let go of all teachers and all teachings, and sit still under the Bodhi Tree until he became enlightened.

So we can see that these teachings have always been with us in known history, yet few there are who have attained such realization. Now, it is a time where the many will have access to this remembrance, and come to experience a Direct Source Connection from within the sanctum sanctorum of their very own being.

In honor of this Direct Source Connection within each being, the Star Elders & Ancient Ones say repeatedly in the many verbal transmissions coming through, that they are not here to hand us our enlightenment. They cannot "walk up the stairs for us," but they can assist us by reaching out their hand and helping us walk up the stairs, if we in our free will choosing decide to request this assistance.

This book is one of these hands held out. Take it if you will, and may it be a great blessing to you!

Chireya: Early Training & Intention

This kind of communication has never been odd to me, thanks to my early training and my initiation at a very young age into the workings of the inner planes. As a small child I would speak with God, though without any sense of religion, and I would also work on myself with spiritual and shamanic-type processes to clear my aura, heal my emotional wounds and get myself centered in my spiritual essence.

A deep desire to "do things that actually help—not just things that my ego / personality thinks will help" has been a gracious steering mechanism, keeping me always on my toes and alert to the actuality of Divine Assistance as it moves through me on behalf of others, my own unfolding path and the planet. This alertness is part of the cultivation of awareness, which is a hallmark of true spiritual growth, allowing us to "do the good work" on ourselves in service to the whole.

I call myself an Orator and Scribe, sanctioned to bring in these teachings in the most authentic way, which is also in a co-creative manner. I do not call myself a "channel" because there are some particularities of how I work with these energies and transmissions, that feel a bit different from the way many channels are typically understood to work.

You could also call me a "translator," as I am designed to and have practiced translating the frequencies of light and encoded information transmitted to me from these sources when I tune in and say "yes" to receiving them. I have spent decades practicing bringing in the purest of the pure energies, as my desire is to truly be of service in this time of awakening, in ways that actually help.

You may notice there are passages where my own life experience and contextual understanding frames the messaging coming through. And this design is on purpose, to give the reader the best possible means to comprehend these teachings within the framework of our modern world.

I have never been a religious person, yet I have always been deeply spiritual. My first memory of my own "conversations with God" took place at age three. Since age eighteen, I have been trained directly by the Star Elders, Ancient Ones and Masters of the Lineages of Light, First Mother, First Father, Source & the I Am Presence of the Divine Mary Magdalene and Yeshua also known as Jesus the Christ. My earliest direct visit was from Yeshua when I was a teenager, teaching me about right use of sexual energy. Subsequently, Yeshua would guide me to "sit" in his heart so I could calibrate to the highest energies of Light available to me through direct energetic connection.

And as an introduction to the manner of communication that comes through me as a scribe and orator for the Lineages of Light, we can think of the entire "Team of Light" currently embodied on the planet as aspects of the Heart of God here to assist as instruments in the liberation and awakening of humanity. "I," the scribe Chireya, could be seen as bringing in an aspect of "The Mind of the Heart of God," as my specialty is to assist with true "comprehension."

A very advanced level of energy work, akashic records insight and genetic lineage clearing along with clairsentient, clairaudient, and clairvoyant abilities comes through me when working with people to assist in clearing the overlays of consciousness described in this book and helping people calibrate to their full expression.

Tune In

As always, I truly recommend "tuning in" with your own Source within as you read this material, and taking those thoughts, ideas, tools and techniques into the cauldron of your very own intuition, keeping what feels good to and for you, and leaving the rest. The full nature of this teaching and my own life's work, is to empower individuals to discover that Source within, and so it goes even with these teachings coming through, please do "think for yourself," feel for yourself, and know for yourself what resonates and what does not.

Leverage your feelings as a point of curiosity, a launching pad for self-discovery which, in my way of comprehending our existence, is the most powerful and useful type of learning and growth. As an additional idea for contemplation, I recommend taking note if you get "charged" emotionally around any aspect of the material presented. This might represent a stuck spot, a set of beliefs that may or may not serve you at this time. Use this emotional charge to help you dig a little deeper into self examination, reflection and possibly healing work to integrate an aspect of self or "truth" that might feel difficult to integrate, but will assist you in your growth.

Either way, "you da boss!"

I do believe that thousands of people are "calling these teachings forth" so that they can more easily and readily express the healing, gift of service and enlightenment they seek and desire to embody in this lifetime.

I am eternally grateful to the Star Elders, Ancient Ones & Masters of the Light, First Mother, First Father and Source, for their persistent, gentle and strong approach to guiding me over the years, so that these works may be birthed and that the information, insight, processes, techniques and clarity might get to the people who need them.

May we aspire higher, as we learn to activate the Love within our own hearts, the Presence within our own bodies, and the Higher Intelligence within our own minds, so that we can truly become conscious instruments of the Golden Age of Enlightenment, Harmony and Love which is predicted to soon reign supreme on this beautiful earth.

~ Chireya

OPENING MESSAGE

There is only One. One Presence, One Power, One Being. The reality of this knowing is underpinning all of existence in a way that totally eludes the normal mind. The result of past thinking patterns and actions has ultimately caused people to believe in the lie of separateness.

The lie of separateness is believed so strongly that even your science and your educational, organizational structures have endorsed it completely. There is a great divide among you now, as those who choose to awaken begin to remember their unity with all life, and as those who are clinging to duality and a separation-consciousness are polarized into a greater fear.

The truth is, your body and your mind and your heart and your soul are all a part of your eternal nature. There is no death, and there is no end to consciousness. Shapes and forms change constantly in a beautiful dance of refracted imagery, all emanating from the One place, the One being, the One love. Our little minds latch onto these pictures and images and attempt to fractionate them into many parts.

Do you remember the myth of Humpty Dumpty? Humpty Dumpty sat on a wall, Humpty Dumpty had a great fall. All the King's horses and all the King's men couldn't put Humpty together again.

Let's examine this.

"Hum," the great intonation of creation, came to a place of division. This division allowed for a fall in consciousness which fractionated us who were One into us who are many—scattered, fragmented and thinking we are not one.

The King (power, will, rules) and his men (strength, force, control) could not restore this oneness. Does this mean the Oneness is not restorable? No. It simply means the parts of the whole, each of which are innately seeking the restoration of this state of oneness, cannot do it, cannot accomplish it, from the point of view of the fractionated nature. From the fractioned out consciousness, the mind grasps for control, power and rules to set life to order, to put things together again. However, it never seems to work, does it? It always falls short and seems to cause even more suffering. This is because it is not the right way; it is not the right way to put Humpty back together again.

So what is the right way?

How do we re-accomplish what was once a normal state of being?

A state of inner and outer peace reflected in our very nature? This is what these offerings will assist you with if you allow them. Allow yourself to be immersed in the knowing that all is well. As we piece ourselves back together again, we will reintegrate many parts of ourselves and begin to understand what has been lost, and to see what will be regained.

This is a journey of consciousness through suffering, loss, grief, pain and madness into redemption, recalibration, realignment reintegration and finally, peace.

The peace we seek together is a peace which indeed surpasses all the 'understanding' of the mind and which instead restores the deep intrinsic knowing of us as the eyes, ears, arms and expressions of One Profound Life, capable of experiencing great joy, satisfaction, harmony and peace.

Our very process of breaking apart and coming together again can be a joyous one. Even the pain, suffering and trauma from the experience of separation can now be a golden boon, a learning stick, and a guide post on the way back home.

Truly all of it is beloved, all of it is delicious, and all of it can be enjoyed, appreciated and healed as we witness the restorations under way.

For those who resist the process of mass awakening which is now occurring on our planet, the ride may seem more painful.

We will hold these in love and kindness, and we will learn to be ever more gracious, grateful and compassionate as we witness the suffering of others. Truly all are our brothers, all are our sisters, and as we help one another, we help ourselves.

These words are not unfamiliar to you, as they ring in the truth of your own divine soul's knowing. Allow them to unfold and unfurl the wings and the energies inside of you so that you can begin to soar into the heights of your true level. All is well.

~ I AM Sanat Kumara

LOVE'S TRUE POWER

Remember that time as a child when reality felt fresh and exhilarating? Many of you can access these memories. There was a tenderness, an awakeness and an awareness about your being which was the natural state in which you found yourselves.

As you began to interact more and more with the adults and other children around you, you would each have very specific manners in which you would respond or react to the turmoil carried in your midst.

I want you to embrace yourself fully as you realize and remember that you were shocked out of your natural state, into a state of reactivity. This was not an easy time for you.

This was not an easy thing. Because of the love that you naturally are, you simply witnessed, allowed and moved forward. With each shock, there was a repression, or a supression, of some of that tenderness.

It was as if you were trying to protect it from the harshness and sharpness of the world around you.

Some of you had come into lineages where harshness ruled so supremely that you hardly remember the tender energies of your true essence. The reason you became jaded or mean or unkind was because you were vastly insulted by the complete lack of acknowledgment of who you really are, and the goodness, tenderness and love that you are.

Let's just acknowledge this for a minute, and let's allow ourselves to reset a bit, to restore, to realign and to recalibrate. Take a deep breath, relax, and say, "Self, I love you. Self, I am sorry we had to go through that. Self, let's now take a step backwards, a big step backwards, into the empty space of pure divine love from which we emerged and in which we have our true being." You may feel a pulse of electricity, a fear, or a shuddering. You may feel a resistance, or you may feel a wave of pure divine love.

Whatever it is you feel, simply allow it to be there. For the way out, the way back, the way through, is far more simple than our tangled mortal mind can typically comprehend.

The true self we always are, were and will be is always there, underneath, as if buried.

But even this is not a true analogy as there is no thing outside of this true self.

This true self is still the essence of everything included in the experience of separation. It is as if it simply got crunched, cramped, twisted, put in a closet that was too small with other things that did not fit well together.

This crampedness, this compression, simply needs to be unfurled, unwound, loosened and released. So truly our process of coming into oneness is not one of striving, but one of allowing. Allowing the self to shine, to be, to live and to love. We have all heard the great teachings about love. Love is the answer. Love is the greatest teacher. All things have their life in Love. Without love we are nothing. These teachings are all true, and are all indicating the simplicity of the journey home.

In our journey home as we unfurl, we are making our way back through the traumas that caused our compression to begin with. This is why many are experiencing remembrances of past lives, or feelings of ancestral memories from the lineages we are carrying in our DNA.

This unfurling process will untwist and unwind until complete just like a yoyo string will unwind when thrust downward. The impetus and momentum of Creation Itself is the Causative factor for this unfurling. The time is now, the process has begun, and we are each truly here for the ride.

The sages are aware that we can go there kicking and screaming, or we can enjoy the ride. There is no choice of 'not unfurling.' Everyone and everything is on this healing journey together, as everyone and everything is an expression of this same ONE experiencing a timing sequence of completion. Truly what this means is that you can relax, you can allow, you can embrace love as the Causative healing factor of all of existence.

Many of you have fears around what you will do for a living if you simply reside in love, if you simply shine your light. Your ages of compression have led into some very interesting scenarios and adventures including the illusory existence of a money economy which seems to have its own desperate and pulling needs upon you. This experience is very real and we wish to allow you to become aware that even though the experience is real, the backing of it is completely tenuous.

The real backing behind you is the power and love of what you call GOD, LOVE, LIGHT. This is the true nature of your existence, your true currency, your actual Access Card to All That Is, the great database harboring all information called the Akashic Records as well as the portalway to wells of abundance, which are completely unlimited.

Because of the push-pull of the mind and the savviness of the illusionists, you are really made to believe things like money, society's constructs, rules and controls are real, actual, tangible things. The power of your own mind, which is one with the power which created all things, has been led to believe it is a limited, controlled, finite entity which will die and which has no access to universal resources. In all honesty this is quite an astounding feat. It is one of the great outcomes of the time of separation that we will collectively, as one, recall: We were actually able to have an experience of separation from Our Self so profound that it caused these beliefs to run very, very deep in countless beings.

We can marvel at this fact and we can learn from it. Mostly at this point, we can unfurl from it and allow Love to realign our systems, ways and resource models back into harmony, devotion and pure joy. If you do not believe this is possible from your current state of mind heart and being, have mercy upon yourself and know that all is well.

Know that you will begin to realize love's true power as you progress on the path, especially at this particular juncture of our journey. For many of you have been feeling the acceleration of the energies of Light, Love, Harmony and Truth, and you have been having direct experiences of the power of this love. It is as if you are awakening from a deep, deep slumber in which you have experienced many nightmares.

The nightmare of a lack of resources, wealth and money is one which many of you are sharing at this particular time. And we do not say this in this manner to belittle you or your profound experience. We recognize the reality of it as you move through it and this is why we are here to support you in regrouping so that the power of the Love that you are can again take precedence in your mind body and soul over the power of the destructive and tightening energies of constriction from which these money economies and beliefs in lack have come.

It is not a trite affair quickly dealt with necessarily, nor is it wise to underestimate the power of your experience. It is also not prudent to put any energy on an idea that you are somehow not advanced if you do not already full realize this. The very fact that there is an experience of limitation which came from your daily life and living mingled with your collective interchanges means that this is a complex and intricate muddle which must be dealt with, with the appropriate and direct attention it requires to truly rebalance you and bring you back into the fold of the grandest reality.

If you can allow yourself to imagine the longevity of this cycle of compression, beyond the constrictions of the normally accepted historical timelines, you will see that this compression has been building for a very long time. As you have simply begun to cross over into the unfurling portion of this process you will realize there is MUCH to unfurl. At the same time, there is no need to be dampened or worried about how long it will take to restore yourselves, as this is a natural process which will truly take care of itself. Your only true job is to be willing to show up fully and allow the energies of love to heal, enliven, uplift and deliver you.

There are many great adventures ahead as you begin to rest more and more in these energies of love. Your inner barometer will always lead you to the next perfect spot for the unwinding. You see, this whole process is highly synchronized, aligned and perfect in its scientific geometric nature. All beings are portal-ways to other dimensions and experiences, and you each carry key codes for each others awakening.

The use of free will to resist the energies of love here to assist you is something you can of course choose. This typically creates greater pain and suffering than is truly bearable. The easier choice is to allow love to love you as you ride through this ocean. The reason this sometimes feels unbearable itself is because that love begins to hit the constricted places and knots and tangles of past actions, words and deeds.

As it does so, the discomfort and restriction and constriction are actually felt and made actual in the awareness. We often don't realize we are feeling this discomfort BECAUSE love is unwinding it, so we resist the process. We resist the love, we engage in habits that cause a suppression of feeling such as eating, drugs, sex, over activity and all other known addictive behaviors. It is easy to see why this would happen so again; it is good to be compassionate towards Ones self.

There are many of you who are already well on your way on this journey of unwinding, and others who are just beginning. Again, let there be no judgment or 'better than' energy or ideas attached to this realization. Just know that in this process of unwinding, some of you got 'wound up' earlier than others. Therefore on the backwards motion, these ones of you are being unwound seemingly more quickly than the others. It is as if we are making a journey back through time, back through all the suffering that ever happened to cause our current state of separation and therefore one feeling by one instance by one experience we will resolve, release and let go.

Now, this is a very deep teaching and also a very simple one. It is as profound and complicated as it is simple and basic. This is the grand paradox of life. This is why these materials are coming forth at this time along with many others to assist us. We, your elder brothers and sisters, would not leave you without a rope and a tether when we see and understand what you are going through – because we too have gone through these things, these times, this type of unwinding process ourselves and therefore, we do have a true compassion for you in your awakening process. We know it is not always easy or comfortable, and we also know who you are.

THE PROFOUND NATURE OF AWAKENING

This history of your star system and your world is very rich, very deep and very old, much older than you have been lead to believe. Your history is woven into the strands of your DNA like the warp and weft of a very large old tapestry.

Realizing the essence of Goodness which is your true nature takes some doing under these circumstances. If you are in alignment with and in total belief of your own goodness and worthiness, it is much easier to let love love you. When you have beliefs that you are less than perfect, that you have sinned, that you are bad or that you have not fulfilled your mission, it is much more difficult to allow that power of love to caress, soothe, nurture and care for you. Add to that the societal norms and expectations imposed upon you from birth by well meaning relatives, friends and community members. You can begin to understand the delicacy of this juncture where you must take one foot out of the illusion while still believing it's real, and put that foot sharply into the reality while still believing it to be untrue. Quite a conundrum!

This is of course where we bring in the energies of Faith, Trust and Love to assist us in birthing into and through this shift period. Verily we say unto you, there is a net! There is a net. When you do take your foot out of the old, the love that you are will catch you. Life may not look, feel or seem 'normal' or even be normal compared to what others are living, but remember, this is all part of the plan. What is so-called normal has come about through a twisting and compression of your true nature into a restricted place of limitation. Is that really what you wish to continue experiencing?

One of the grandest materializations of this twisting energy is it's ability to make people believe it is so real that they will do things counter to their very own intuition and inner knowing, even going to lengths of harming others in order to uphold the beliefs so birthed. Again let us marvel at the feat this is that has been accomplished. We wish to instill deeply the realization that compassion for yourself as you make your way through this matrix of illusion is truly in order. Therefore we want to acknowledge you for your great acts of courage as you step through the hoops of fire and do what you are guided to do from Love over choosing to do those things the illusion is calling you to do. This is no small feat. We of the Star Councils of Elders are in true witness of you and your process as one by one by one you are choosing love over fear and turning the tides for yourselves and your planet.

There is a profound awakening emerging now, and it will only become more apparent as time goes on. Those of you who are reading this material are the harbingers of this new era. You are the space holders and awakeners who will be assisting as the masses begin to stir in their sleep. It has not been an easy journey for you in your dedication to jump in first and hold space for this process as you have had to go through it alone without the resources with which the many will be blessed as they begin to awaken. For you and others before you have seeded this time with your love so that you can bear witness to the grand awakening and hold space for your siblings as they unwind.

The most profound implication here is that all is well. This is a radical concept from certain points of view. How can all be well with so much suffering in the world? Now as we begin to understand the nature of love and the nature of the compression and constriction that has occurred to mask loves' presence, it is easier to realize that indeed all is well, all will be well, and everything that needs healing will be healed.

So rest in love my dear ones. Rest in love's embrace and allow yourselves to melt.

What is melting is the old remnants of a belief in a self that was less than perfect, less than lovable, less than whole, less than complete.

Allow the pain and suffering, loss and fear to melt away for you, and as you do so, begin to realize that this same melting is now happening for millions and millions of other beings, whether or not it is yet apparent. Allow this deepening feeling and expression of love to evoke a truer and truer compassion for all beings who are with you on this journey of spirit and awakening.

As you do so, you align with the dominant energies on the planet, the energies of light, awakening, goodness, growth and well being.

The mass consciousness awakening is a joyful sight to behold from the inner planes.

From this perspective it is as if sets upon sets of Christmas tree lights which had once been broken begin to illuminate randomly one by one. We see the lights come on and we see the peace begin to take precedence over worry, fear and anxiety in people's lives.

Everyone knows 'something is up.' All the programmed information about doomsday, Armageddon and the end of the world have had an impact on consciousness.

Simultaneously the very real and obvious problems of your current time frame give credence to those types of thought forms because of the extreme nature of the pollution, corruption and greed prevalent on the planet.

What most have not yet done is to make the shift directly into the heart, into the cosmic consciousness of awakening. We are like harbingers of a new vibration, illuminators of a new way, simply guiding you as you access your own deep inner knowing about who you truly are and what your role is on the planet at this time. This is not a process to be feared. However, there may be moments when you do feel afraid. Simply know that all is well as you pass through gateway by gateway by gateway into a new vibration altogether.

The technology of awakening has many aspects on many dimensions. When an awakening sequence begins on a planet, there are runners sent ahead to embrace the current culture by living within it, yet still carrying the seed frequencies of a more expanded consciousness.

These beings often suffer in their earthly experience, yet they know they have a purpose and a mission to fulfill.

They often do not fully awaken in their given life time as they are simply there to sow and spread this divine ray of love, forgiveness and peace without necessarily being fully aware of their function at the time. As the mass consciousness begins to attune little by little to these new energies, more and more light is opened up in different parts of the world, and certain places become citadels of higher consciousness where more of like mind and heart are attracted.

This is a normal part of a time sequencing of preparing a culture for the energies of awakening and it takes hundreds if not thousands of years. There is a grand procession of events and orchestrations to lift everyone into the kind of moment we are now experiencing on earth. Your planet's history is deep and rich, deeper and richer than you can even imagine.

The cycles of forgetfulness and awakening have been numerous. On a soul level you have all been through this before. And so in the deepest chambers of your being there is a comfort and a knowing even as you go through the discomfort of shifting from polarity and duality back into unity. Simply know that all is well.

As beings begin to awaken more and more, you will find yourself holding a new space of love for those around you. As you personally embrace the energies of love, peace and harmony which are now more fully available to you, you will see transformation in your personal life. Being attached to the mythologies of your current day culture of how things ought to be will only lead to a slowing down of the process of transformation. For truly the systems and energetics of your current collective experience are less than fully awakened, less than fully worthy of your stature as divine beings. Even so, you have been programmed and seeded in this life to believe in the mainstream materialistic lifestyle of getting, having and establishing yourself in acceptable ways.

Simply know that this is a process, and what will be unfolding for you individually and collectively is as yet fresh, new and unknown. So allow yourself to simply be present to what is real for you, what is up for you, at any given moment. There will be days when you may feel panicky about needing more funds or not feeling in alignment with what you should be accomplishing or being according to normal standards.

And there will be days when you feel the rush and light and love of fresh new energies like never before. These energies can be exhilarating, and can help you establish the trust field within yourself and with your own Source connection which will assist you in a smoother transition. The transition from love to fear can be as fun as we allow it to be. It is also a time for deep compassion for self and others. Since you have been through this life time on earth with all its compression and anxiety and anger patterns, you know first hand the kinds of subtle or gross suffering everyone has been through. It does not feel good to feel separate, be made wrong, or chastised in any way. In fact, it is not in your true nature to have these experiences. So part of you is still deeply saddened that you have had to endure these types of things, while part of you is very strong and aware that love will eventually heal it all.

YOUR COSMIC CALLING CARD

We celebrate you on your path of awakening. We are here for you always. All you have to do is rest upon your inner quietude and ask for the love that you are to assist you, to uplift you, to show you the way. Learning to pay attention to the answers sent forth from this love that you are is the greatest gift you can give yourself. For truly as the great ones have said, when you ask you shall receive. So how do we hear the answers in a world of distractions? We begin to practice an inner quietude and expansion of awareness which will allow you to feel, see, know, sense or hear the answers from your Source.

How do we do this? There are many possible ways, and we will give you a few of these ways now to help ground the experience of receiving the true guidance you are seeking.

EXERCISE:
Accessing the Love Within You for Guidance

1. Let's imagine you are sitting on a mountain top in a beautiful expansive region. You can go to

this place in your mind and bring in all your feelings and senses. What does the air smell like? Are there birds or animals about? What time of day is it? How does the ground feel under you? Are you comfortable? What would make you more comfortable? Bring in the things that would make you more comfortable in this vision.

2. Now as you are sitting still on your imaginary mountain top, begin to breathe very deeply. Begin to notice those places of constriction in your body. Really allow yourself to notice where you are holding tension, and where you are relaxed and your energies are flowing. Pass no judgment upon yourself for having these tight spots. For truly it is how it is, because it is how it is. There is no judgment. You have been through the separation experience and therefore you have received constrictions and repressions which are now being resolved. Have compassion for yourself. Love yourself.

3. Now imagine within your heart there is a light shining very brightly. Allow this light in the center of your heart to glow and glow and grow bigger and bigger. As this glowing sun in the

middle of your heart begins to glow more and more brightly, know that all is well.

4. Allow this light to begin to spread in a spherical manner into and through your whole body and out into your aura. This light will begin to cleanse your aura and your body and your consciousness. You will begin to notice places of discomfort which can be witnessed into release simply by allowing the light to continue to penetrate there.

5. Now as your entire aura is filled with this beautiful golden white light from your heart area, simply rest in the void of this light.

6. Simply state to yourself that you release all pain, all discomfort and all sadness into this light.

7. Simply state that you release all grief, all anger and all fear into this light.

8. Ask this Light and this Love to please guide you, to please show you the way that is the highest and best way for you in your life and living now. If you experience emotions such as crying, sadness, or any other emotion at all, simply know that all is well and that you are being

healed. This release is what is needed in order to loosen up the flows of energies in your system.

You are a beautiful God being now awakening and you deserve the utmost respect of yourself and of life. Even if those around you cannot yet recognize your beauty and your light, still know that Life Itself recognizes you, witnesses you, and holds you in true compassion and understanding. Simply become aware that these others who cannot yet see you are only in this state because of their own suffering, their own experience of the separation. Therefore know that all is well, and that as you simply embrace yourself and them in the love that you are, unconditionally, they too will have a better opening for beginning to shift.

As you rest within this light and this love, you may also ask this light and love to give you very specific signals that you can personally recognize in your daily life when the guidance is being offered, when the answers are coming through.

"Get through to me, easily gently and in peace!" is one such command you can offer.

Truly there are myriad beings who are more fully immersed in this light and this love than you are at current, who are here witnessing you, ready to assist you. You do not necessarily need to know their names, for truly, we are all one with the great

Source energy that births and is this light and love. And so as witnesses to this love and this light, the guides who are assisting you will humbly and joyfully offer you service in the name of the One that we are.

You see we each have our own personal vibration, our personal signature within the embrace of the great One in which we all truly have our being. One helpful way to visualize this is to imagine a large crystalline sphere with innumerable facets. Imagine that this sphere is not sold yet is faceted even underneath the outer facets all the way to its core.

Each one of these shiny facets represents a being, an aspect of the One represented by the whole sphere. The light shines through and reflects upon each of these facets at a unique angle, giving each being their own special signature, perspective and energy template. This may be likened unto your Cosmic Calling Card, so that in all of creation the Creator that is our One Source knows and recognizes each being, each plant, each planet, each bug, and each animal as itself. This is mysterious in that it is mind-boggling to imagine how this can be possible with trillions upon trillions of beings throughout all the universes; however it is true.

You are unique, special and precious, beloved of the One that birthed you. Your Cosmic Calling

Card is your ticket to your Source connection. Through it you can access everything you need to access in order to grow and aspire to your own greatest heights in this lifetime.

How do you use your Cosmic Calling Card to gain access to what you need? There are many ways.

Let's do another exercise.

EXERCISE:
Accessing Your Cosmic Calling Card

1. This time, quiet yourself and imagine you are living in the center of this great faceted sphere representing the One and all created beings.

2. Simply breathe in and out as you rest within the heart of the One.

3. Allow the love and light of the One to gently breathe you in and throughout all of creation through the visual metaphor of these facets.

4. Feel the deep relaxation and peace as you do this. Rest here a moment and simply breathe in and out this love and this light through all of creation represented in this imagery.

5. You will begin to notice that your holographic awareness of the entire sphere includes the awareness of all the facets. While you may not be able to read all the facets at once, you can begin to see and feel that if you were to place your awareness on any single facet, you will be able to detect a certain feeling, thought, vibration or essence of this being.

6. Now shift your awareness to another facet and see/feel/know how this is different from the facet before. Play with this, moving your consciousness from facet to facet. There is no right or wrong experience as you begin to play with feeling the different Cosmic Calling Cards of the various beings in creation.

7. Now go back within the center again of this divine primal source energy sphere with many facets. Breathe in and out from the center once again, allowing your consciousness to softly include all the facets while resting on no one facet in particular.

8. Rest here in this awareness for a moment.

9. And now ask this overlighting One Source also called God, Love, etcetera, to direct you to your

own particular facet, to the facet through which you are experiencing creation in this lifetime.

10. In your mind's eye, you may be directed to see this facet which represents you. Notice any special colors, any distortions, any feelings you may get as you rest your attention upon your special vibration. Now imagine yourself as inside looking out. How does it feel? What is your vibration? What does it feel like, look like? Does it feel as if the energies of this facet are flowing smoothly, or are there blockages?

11. Begin to get to know your own vibration. When we are living through the awareness of our own vibration, we might not always be totally aware of it and it's uniqueness.

12. Feel into this vibration and perhaps take some notes, or make a drawing of it. What colors come to mind? What are the elements that are most potently alive in you? Fire, air, water, earth, ether?

13. As you become more familiar with your own vibration, you can also ask this One Source Light that we are in our totality to show you the particular aspects of your vibration which might

be cloudy, shut off, or out of alignment with your original pattern. This might come to you in visual form, or in a feeling, a word or a sensation. You might hear words about the nature of any imbalances and you may begin to receive guidance upon how to restore your vibrational blueprint to its original integrity.

You see, as we have passed through the ages of the separation, we have all picked up varying degrees of distortions that have made us feel slightly out of kilter with ourselves, our surroundings or our loved ones. This is also natural and not to be judged. Simply know that now is the appointed time where we begin to throw off vibrations that are not true to our core nature, and reveal more fully our original essence and expression of Self as pure divine aspects of the One.

This process is kind of like God playing hide and seek, like God playing dress up. First God made the illusion of being many instead of one, and then further added to the disguise by donning unusual frequencies or energetic outfits so that we could play a game of being something other than who and what we really are. Now, the game is coming to a close, and we are beginning to change clothes back into the fresh, light and love filled energies of our original nature. You could call it a cosmic strip tease as one by one by one we begin to shed our outworn outfits and reveal the beauty of our naked truth. Enjoy the process! Even with the emotional flare ups, the upsets, and the rampages of outworn vibrations we can enjoy the process of revealing our true Self to ourselves.

What would it be like, feel like, sound like, if we were restored to our true original vibration? Rest in this feeling again and take any notes or make any pictures that come to mind. In this revelation will be hints about who we are and what our true roles are at this particular juncture of the journey.

Once you have reestablished your connection with your own personal Cosmic Calling Card, what can you do with it? What is its purpose and function? Well, of course on a very basic level, its purpose is to distinguish you as a unique facet of the One, endowed with attributes which assist you in fulfilling your particular destiny and playing your particular role in the grand play of creation.

The world as we know it has offered a vibration which suggests that you are a burden to a system, which is more important to you, and that you must therefore strive to figure out how to serve this system so that you can be worthy of receiving life support. This is the perspective of pure illusion. Nothing could be further from the truth. Some of you have been hit with this vibrational offering harder than others.

Feelings of unworthiness, of having to make up for your presence on the planet by acts of servitude, feelings of being less than whole, less than good, or needing to justify your existence all stem from this illusory offering.

On the other hand, some of you have been experiencing a more grandiose vibration which puts you squarely in charge of others, superior, and therefore more worthy than others of the good life has to offer.

Separating the so called good from the bad, the beautiful from the ugly, the rich from the poor, the wise from the dumb, has been the function of duality in creating this intrinsic illusion which has wreaked so much havoc on the ecology, economy and communities of this world.

Your existence is supported by Life Itself because you are a part of Life Itself.

You do not have to prove yourself to become worthy of love, food, care or goodness. The systems of your planet modeled upon this scarcity complex and this sense of separation have caused a veritable energetic blockage, a traffic jam of consciousness which has disallowed the full good that is yours to get to you easily in this lifetime.

Likewise, the system as it has been created has flowed to you all kinds of things that you truly do not need and require to live a full and happy life. In fact, many of these things, items, belongings, thought forms, relationships, vibrations, institutional communions, become outright blockages to experiencing who you truly are, and what you truly require to live a life of joy.

Most of you will find that a simple life filled with love, positive relationships, opportunities to give your special talents and gifts and opportunities to receive the special talents and gifts of others in a beautiful natural setting with foods that come directly from nature and time to play, relax and enjoy the planet you are on is all you truly require and desire. From that place of relaxation and joy many great gifts of service, insight, higher technology and true change-agent assistance for your planet can come through you.

So if you are feeling a desire to simplify, a desire to be released from certain patterns, habits, things, relationships, situations, objects, plans and ideas, know that all is well and that this feeling is guiding you toward the joy you deserve to live.

As you clean up your personal vibration on an energetic or spiritual level, you will see that it becomes easier and easier to release that which is not you, that which is not for you, of you or by you in your own personal divine plan. You will become more attractive to and more attracted by those people, places and things which truly serve, acknowledge, respect, honor and delight you. You will become more willing to be delighted, honored, respected and appreciated. You will become more willing to receive goodness, truth, purity, simplicity and the kind gifts of nature.

Imagine the impact as each one of you begins to shed the trappings of the old world. There is vibrational permission at this time to shed these outworn attributes, which you may not have felt in the previous times of your life. There is ever increasing energetic support for you in shifting your vibration, your choices and your lifestyle as more and more love and light are returning to your planet.

Imagine how the shift will occur now that we are considering these things. What if each of you just simply released and let go of the fear based contracts, obligations, and relationships with organizations, institutions and people who are still entrenched in contracted energies of lack and duality? What will happen as more and more love and light are able to pour through you, a facet of the One with a particular frequency and particular gifts? These true gifts will be able to shine forth more lucidly.

They are already there, they already exist. You do not need to DO anything to create the gifts that you hold; they are already created. You simply learn to rest in the oneness and love that you are, allowing it to wash away all that is not needed from your field, your consciousness and your reality, while paying attention to the light-filled impulses to action you feel during this process.

As you act on these impulses, ever increasing light and love will begin to flow through. Increasingly, ease and grace will come to you in pursuit of your own truth in action. More and more love will flow through your vessel and your life, helping you to become even more attractive to the like vibrations of love, beauty, nurturance and support that you are personally embodying.

A question may be arising in you now, around how that can be the case when we still have an entire money economy in place in which we are entangled and which seems so strongly to be at the foundation of our life and living?

This is something we wish to address with you very deeply to assist you in creating and bringing in the bridge-ways from the old to the new that help you feel balanced as you move into your true vibrations.[1]

Support for Your Vibration

The age of separation itself has set into motion an array of components which are directly contrary to your true nature and the true manner in which reality supports you.

This array of components are very convincing even while being completely illusory.

We will be addressing these components one by one so that you can begin to dismantle them and release them thus restoring your true foundation of support in your earthly experience, which exists across all time.

COMPONENT 1
Belief you are Evil, Wrong or Bad

COMPONENT 2
Belief in lack, limitation and scarcity ("scare city")

COMPONENT 3
Belief that you owe your existence to someone or some thing, some country or some institution and

---

[1] See Appendix 1: Resources for ways to access further assistance

therefore must pay either financially, emotionally, through labor, or in some other way to 'make up for' the space you are taking up on the planet

COMPONENT 4
Belief that you must do as your fore parents have done. Often this one is subtle and hidden.

COMPONENT 5
Belief in your educational precepts which have indicated a false human history, placing you within that history in an erroneous way.

COMPONENT 6
Belief that you are disconnected from your Source Energy and that you do not have direct access to All That Is, all resources, all love and all light.

The manner in which these components have been embedded into your conscious and unconscious belief systems has been traumatic in and of itself.

So, an additional aspect of this clearing we wish to address is:

COMPONENT 7
Emotional Trauma caused by the embedding of all components over time, and in your genetic lineages

We are outlining for you these aspects of your collective experience layer by layer so that you can begin to feel into the holographic nature of reality and begin to access directly all this information straight from the Unified Field.

This will come to you more easily and readily as you immerse yourself in the power and presence of Love and Light, releasing judgment, fear and preconceptions. The direct access to the Unified Field of All Consciousness, All Love, All Light, All Data and All Truth is one of your birthrights as a Divine Being of the One That Is. We wish to help restore you in full consciousness and experience unto this birthright. An examination of each of these components and what you can do to dissolve each one is offered in these writings.

COMPONENT ONE:
Belief you are Evil, Wrong or Bad

The many religious patterns and precepts which have built upon your consciousness and the consciousness of your ancestors over time which have been falsely based in an idea akin to an 'original sin' or an original badness have been deeply embedded not only in consciousness and the mental/emotional bodies of the people of this planet but also in your cellular structures.

These patterns do get passed on from generation to generation until someone in the lineage comes into the awareness of being able to cleanse and clear them out.

The idea of original sin perpetrated into the Abrahamic lineages has mirroring energies in the other religions of the world.

There is a grave misunderstanding in most if not all religions about the nature of evil, the nature of duality and the nature of beings and God. These misunderstandings have led to misinterpretations which became propagated on a mass scale through time and space.

Indeed, these misperceptions have even been leveraged by those beings who have reveled in the separation causing anxiety and fear in order to manipulate and control other beings for their own purposes. Surely we say to you this cycle is coming to an end, so fear not! Know that all is well and rest in a state of union and inner peace even as you shed the old for the new.

Know that even those who have been entrenched by the tappings of greed, fear, lust, power and control over others are also part of the One and are making their way home as well, albeit perhaps at a different pace seemingly from you or others who are fully released of any desire to control, harm or manipulate others for greedy purposes.

You see, long ago, when the spiritual teachings were coming to this planet, the consciousness of all those receiving them was not totally ripe for digesting the truths in their core essence.

Fear and a disconnected state combined with these teachings led to precepts[2] which are completely antithetical to the reality of your true nature as a being of Love. The great lie taught you that you came in tainted and are not worthy of goodness and love, but that you have to earn it through some type of suffering or slavery/servitude.

The precept of Original Sin comes from the experience of a disconnection from the Source of all life and that this disconnection experience has been passed on from generation to generation.

It is revelatory in nature. Instead of saying you are wrong, bad and evil, with 'sin' in you, the teaching was indicating the nature and state of things as existing in a state of separation from God Consciousness. If we go to the original core essence of this offering, we will see that it merely reveals that we have been cut off and that the path of aspiration is one of total and complete restoration of the

---

[2] See glossary of terms for explanation of the use of "Precept"

consciousness of Self as intrinsically one with Life, Love, God and All Goodness.

In the twisted mindset of separation, greater pain was inflicted upon an original pain. Believing that you have come in unworthy, and receiving that reflection not only through words, but through the daily habits, acts and tendencies of those around you, this basic belief that you are somehow bad, wrong or evil became increasingly engrained. Each soul has been evolving, growing, learning and throwing off these patterns at varying rates over many lifetimes. Various lineages of people have also been releasing these patterns little by little over time.

Now we are at a juncture where the collective consciousness can begin to throw off this belief en masse. Of course it does need to be released on all levels, spiritually, emotionally, mentally, and physically.

Many people can reject the belief system entirely, becoming 'spiritual and not religious' or even atheist, rejecting religion along with a sense of God, yet still feel in their emotional bodies a deep sense of unworthiness. That is because by our holographic nature, imprints or programs become systemic and therefore need to be resolved and rooted out systemically as well. As one energy body clears it becomes easier and easier for all energy bodies to fully clear the belief system.

The energetic reaction to carrying this belief in original sin and 'badness' shows up differently in different people.

Because at a core level we know we are good and worthy, some of us have a reaction of anger at anything that looks or feels akin to the 'thing' that suggests otherwise.

This is the case where people reject any sense of spirit whatsoever in an attempt to throw off the unwanted pattern.

Of course this is the essence of throwing the baby out with the bath water and will only take a person so far. It is easy to see the large amounts of anger still held in the emotional body of the field because of the presence of this pattern. You can therefore see why it becomes important to allow the patterns to clear from all four energy bodies so that they can be released entirely, and so that the being can be free to rediscover his or her natural, unique and authentic connection to the source of life, by whatever name they choose to call it.

A complementary energy pattern which may be on the surface of consciousness or hidden away that is associated with a basic belief in being evil, wrong or bad is a pattern of fearing God, feeling punished by God, and believing in life as an ongoing punishment for our 'sins'.

The truth is, our lack of Source connection itself causes an experience of a lack of flow and grace which may in fact show up and appear to be a form of punishment. We can assure you once and for all that the Prime Creator of All Life is not about punishment at all.

There is no thing akin to punishment in the mind and heart of God. God is pure love, pure joy, pure delight.

And now that we can intellectually comprehend and accept this fact, we must go about the business of extracting the opposing beliefs from all the energy bodies of our being.

Here is one such offering to set in motion the complete clearing of Component One:

EXERCISE:
Complete Clearing of Component 1

- Let us forgive all of our ancestors and relatives, all of our cultural collective and all of our institutions that have perpetrated these thought forms and carried them forward.

- Let us also forgive ourselves for having been party to them. Let us call upon the Spirit of Life and ask to be washed clean of such beliefs on all levels

- Please Creator, please Light, Life and Love, thank you for releasing me from the grips of a belief in original sin, badness and evilness of my own nature.

- Please restore fully my consciousness to the realization of my true divine nature as pure love, At One with your life always.

- Creator please help all beings to forgive me for ever having embodied a belief that you might wish to punish me, or that you might see me as less than perfect and whole.

- In this way Creator, we return ourselves unto our original vibration.

- Please Creator restore our consciousness, mind, body and spirit to its original wholeness and wellness.

- Release us from the past and show us how to love ourselves, how to love one another, how to forgive one another, and how to receive this love.

- Bring into our beings our belief and knowing of our intrinsic goodness and ensure that every cell of our body and every face of our mind and every layer of our emotions and every dimension of our spirits are completely and totally cleared of this belief system based on separation, greed and fear.

- Thank You God ~ Creator ~ Source, Thank You God, Thank You God. Thank You for setting us free.

Restoring Foundational Support for Your Vibration in Component 1

You are a God Being, a Good Being.
You are made of Love, therefore you are Love.

No matter what you have done of a negative nature in the past, it has come from the collective experience of separation. The days of retribution and punishment are over. There is a new order established unto you which is the order of Pure Divine Love, Forgiveness and Healing.

This Order will restore you entirely, will allow you to see the nature of the karmic interactions which have played out in the past, and will finally allow you to lay down your sword which you once wielded against self and other in order to be the beacon of love, light and kind compassion which you truly are. Forgive yourself. Forgive yourself.

All beings who have attempted to punish you or who have punished you have been subject to this same form of shaming, blaming, and separation consciousness mingled with beliefs in punishment, loss and lack.

All beings have played out and perpetrated these harmful ways because of their own core wound of separation.

Therefore we can forgive all beings and ask our Divine Creator to assist in restoring everyone and everything to wholeness at this time. All of creation awaits your triumphant return to the intrinsic knowing of your total goodness. Goodness and the knowing of it is not of the ego or separated illusory consciousness.

The separated illusory consciousness may grasp onto even truths such as this oneness with god in a grandiose manner which is not based in the reality of love. In it you will still feel a vibration of separation and stagnation which will feel 'off kilter' to you.

Simply know that the illusory separated consciousness we call the ego is also on it's way back home. "Argue not with your enemies" is often a good guide stick.

When you are aware of your own or other's ego flaring up, continue seeing and speaking with the soul of the person.

Find the words and vibrations and manners of speech and action which keep you in the vibration of love, wholeness, simplicity, humility and trust.

In this way, you can a) keep your own vibration pure and therefore safe, attracting like vibrations, and b) witness the eventual transformation of even the most stubborn of egos as love's magic unwavering and unconditional power gets to the root of all things and restores us all unto itself.

COMPONENT TWO
Belief in Lack, Limitation and Scarcity

When you look about you in the natural world, observe the trees, the flowers and the animals. When an ecosystem is in harmony, do you notice any lack of anything? Trees reproduce in total abundance, exponentially.

The balancing energies of nature offer and maintain a perfect equilibrium that allows there to be plenty of nourishment, space and energy for all.

Doesn't it follow then that humans, as parts of the Grand Whole, as part of nature, would also be in their natural state abundantly supplied?

What is to keep us from restoring ourselves unto this natural state? Only the beliefs that the systems we have created which birth limitation and lack are somehow superior, or necessary, or correct.

As the collective consciousness of humanity begins to come into alignment and agreement with the principles of natural life and 'reality,' the orderly sequence of events to ensue will surely include a rebalancing of all that is off kilter and a supplying of all true and harmonious need.

Contrary to the popular belief, we do not need so many of the things being produced on this planet at this time. We have a deeply entrenched belief that we require these things in order to thrive. In addition we have technologies and conveniences that may be useful. However, they are being created in a manner which offers more pollution to the planet upon which we live.

This is, when we look at it rightly, not at all a sustainable scenario. Death and disease are surely the outcome of living so far out of kilter with the natural systems of the planet. Just as surely, a return to a simpler way of being and of life causes the scales to reset and the balance to be restored.

Some of you may be resisting this idea because it is believed that our human family has suffered greatly in the past without these vast conveniences we now call normal.

The truth is, it is possible to have technologies that cause great convenience, ease and grace in life without causing harm and damage to the people and the planet. We will discuss some of these technologies in an upcoming chapter.

In the meantime, it is enough to simply know that ceasing to harm oneself with damaging foods, ceasing as much as personally possible to pollute the planet with dangerous fumes and chemicals and taking day by day action steps to come back into alignment with the natural world are action steps that will surely make the needed difference.

One by one by one, as we each make subtle and grand changes in these arenas, it opens the way for more enlightened practices to emerge. In the meantime, the relief of the burden of 'all of that stuff' will begin to stimulate the feeling of inner freedom which will allow you to feel more fully into what is truly yours to do and offer and give at this beautiful and powerful juncture on the planet.

The overuse of resources for things not truly needed and desired has greatly come about in a vain attempt to fill the void experienced because of the disconnection from love and consciousness.

We can understand then with compassion why we have had these practices of greed, overeating and over-consumerism. It is the tender heart indeed which can forgive the errors of he past and see clearly why they have been made to begin with. The deep longing for goodness, for fulfillment and for connection through love with all that is, is always at the core of every issue and challenge.

From this perspective we can see that the perception of shortage, lack or limitation comes as a direct boomerang from the overuse of resources and feelings of unworthiness.

As we practice overuse of resources, this stimulates feelings of unworthiness even further causing more despair and more grasping for things, actions, and food to fill this void.

Somewhere the cycle must end and it won't be completely healed through strict discipline or forcing ourselves to change. This over-strictness can further compound feelings of unworthiness and cause us to feel ashamed of ourselves.

Feelings of shame send us further away from loves embrace and disallow the full integration of the message change has in mind.

Support for Your Vibration in Component 2

- The message is, you are loved and you are love

- You are the bright star shining in the eternal now.

- You have direct access to the Source of all goodness, and you are a harbinger of change.

- Through your actions, words and deeds, you can be an inspiration to many on this path of transformation.

- The message is also that you have the capacity to create, enjoy and bring forth all the pleasure, goodness, deliciousness and love you care to experience in this physical dimension. To do so from a place of full heart centered love will disallow any negative or harmful vibrations to enter into your creations whatsoever.

The polarities of scornful miserliness and overly strict discipline match upon the opposite end of the pendulum swing with destructive over-consumption and greedy ego centered accumulation.

    As we restore ourselves to the harmony and love of our true natures, little by little, we will wash away these extremes both in our personal lives and in our world. For the outer world is a reflection of he inner world, and scarcity is only possible because of the existence of its opposite, over-consumption. We each have a vitally important role to play in restoring the balance.

What if each person began to rebalance acts of consumption and collection in their daily lives within the cauldron of their own heart's knowing and connection to pure positive Source energy?

We can see from this vantage point how the individual behavior impacts the collective reality.

COMPONENT THREE
Belief That You Owe Your Existence To Someone or Some Thing

Belief that you owe your existence to someone or some thing, some country or some institution and therefore, you must pay either financially, emotionally, through labor, or in some other way to 'make up for' the space you are taking up on the planet

Service is not servitude. Servitude is born of the old paradigm of separation, division and suffering. Service is the essence of your true joy, for each Being of God has been created to give of itself in uniquely beneficial and amazing, joyful ways.

Your existence on this planet is your natural birthright and you do not need to have money, energy or work extracted from you in order to be worthy of being here.

The energies of force and control used to perpetrate various kinds of servitude onto our human family in the name of corporate greed have caused an equal and opposite reaction of a) resistance to work, b) resistance to giving, and c) feeling like it is a chore or a burden to help and to give of time and effort.

It has also perpetuated the illusion that we must be paid in money in order to give something to another.

On the flip side, the natural essence of each being strongly desires to give of itself. This is how nature works. Nature is a system of giving and receiving, always operating in perfect flow and harmony. Likewise, doesn't it make sense that the human community would have within its blueprint this very same energy of cohesion, sharing, and direct experiential giving and receiving as a foundation to it's very nature? How do we get 'back' to that natural state from the seeming mess we've made with our commerce, our monetary systems, and our insistence upon certain professions, possessions, indulgences and repressions being a necessary part of life?

As we clear out the remnants of vibrational ugliness which caused us to believe that giving is painful, we will begin to experience our greatest possible joy, the joy of showing up as our true selves to deliver the goods, feelings, insights, ideas and actions which fill us full to overflowing as we give.

This is the true nature of Life Itself. Does a tree hold back from giving oxygen? Would the river stop from flowing? Would birds hinder their own singing for fear of not being taken care of by life unless they charged for the song?

Of course not. We are in a place of beauty wherein we can reorient our conscious awareness to be in harmony with reality instead of being in harmony with illusion.

The illusion says, you need money to survive. People must think a certain thing of you in order for you to be okay and accepted. You must behave a certain way to get ahead in life. We tell you verily these are mere illusions which have nothing to do with reality and how life really works.

There is a great juncture ahead where the scenarios of entrapment through false money economies will be dissolved away like dust in the wind. Fear not as this time approaches, for you will have plenty of time to regroup, reorient and begin to serve a different master, called Love.

The systemic restructuring of an entire planetary economy is underway though it may not be obvious on the outside. Can you imagine life on other planets where the mere idea of having to pay to live on your home planet is completely absurd? The deep entrenchment of belief in the systems which are in place on your planet precludes often the common sense to allow you to realize how falsely used you have been by those who seek to manipulate.

The purpose of this work is not to expose or revile those who have been so deeply entrenched in duality that they have desired to control and harm you in these ways. For just as surely as the sun sets and rises, these too shall awaken as you are doing now and shall renounce the ways of the past. The purpose of bringing up the subject of the maligners has to do merely with assisting you in wiping the dust from your eyes that you might see clearly. The confusing energies of deception and control for greedy purposes have left an imprint that we have many of us become attached to. We really do believe in these systems which hold us captive. We really do rely on their veracity in our daily living, and we really can witness the power of collective belief through the experiences we all have on a daily basis.

The purpose of this treatise is equally not to judge the systems we are discussing, but to bring to light the deep level of programming to which you have been subjected, so that as each one of you desires to regain your cosmic hook up with the actual Source of all life, power and wisdom which is universal, unlimited, unnamable and all powerful, showering you continuously with light love and acceptance, you will be able to understand exactly where you and your communities are in this process and how you can leverage the twin powers of unconditional love and refined discernment to navigate successfully and bountifully through the changes at hand.

Affirmations for Supporting Your Vibration In Component 3

- The love that I am supports me.

- The love that I am nourishes me.

- The love that I am guides me.

- The love that I am carries me through.

- All needs and desires which come from my true heart's joy will always be supported.

- I now ask Love, Light, Creator, The One to assist me in restoring my Divine Alignment with those needs and desires which are a real and authentic aspect of my true nature for my greatest benefit at this particular juncture on my path. Please and Thank you, God.

COMPONENT FOUR
Belief that you must do as your fore-parents have done

Imagine a planetary system and family of humanity out of kilter with its true nature of love and it's true dharma of sharing from the heart the gifts of each one.

If we look at the long term of this situation from the eagle's eye view, we can see that there are levels and layers affecting individuals as they attempt to change. The level of the genetic lineage is one of the most potent change-stoppers because of the immense pressure from birth families to tow the line. As we are aware, many souls are able to break free to varying degrees and to come to do what is in their own personal blueprint, offering more of their true and natural essence to the world.

We can tell by the number of movies on the subject of the youngster having to go through a hero's journey to break away from family patterns which are not in alignment with their soul's life and living that this is indeed a deep archetypal construct and must be operating within us in ways more subtle and gross than we might commonly imagine.

Imagine a baby being born into a human family. This baby is coming from pure Source energy, from God.

While this baby may have its own past life karmas and imprints it must encounter and resolve in this life time, this little one is also now facing the family history of this particular lineage.

There may be many gifts of the lineage encoded in the nervous system and DNA of this little one, gifts because of which the soul chose to incarnate through that particular lineage. At the same time, there may be challenges in store because of the dysfunctions residing within the lineage. The baby is coming from love into a world where there is love yet there is also fear, there is also the consciousness of division and the patterns of lack, limitation and scarcity.

The family of origin may deeply desire to assist this one in being successful, yet, because of their own programming, they may be less than fully capable of reading the signs and signals of these inner impulses with a great enough clarity to truly assist this being.

The advanced human will seek to understand the unique strengths and gifts of the child thus born, and to support this child unwaveringly in the development of these gifts and talents, following solely the interest and energy of the child in these pursuits.

A less advanced lineage holder might see the gifts yet make an interpretation leading to a desire to control or force the child into certain lines of study or discipline. This forcing can also cause resistance in the child to its own gifts.

A less advanced being will not be able to see the natural gifts of the child, and will instead impose upon it the trade, ideas, aspirations and habits of the lineage, and may become very angry when the child expresses a desire to do different things in life.

This of course makes everyone feel worse, and causes more feelings of unworthiness and failure to emerge. The parents feel they have failed because they are having a hard time helping the child to accept their rule and their will.

The child will feel it's a failure because a) it is not pleasing its parent and b) it is also not fulfilling its true destiny. Often a human child is made to choose between a) or b), resulting in an ever lingering sense of failure or lack until the child has a chance to clear this through its own self-selected healing work.

We can see from this vantage point that the parents, even though they may have been acting from anger, frustration and control, were attempting to do their best to help the child.

The child, though perhaps becoming rebellious and leaving the family, or worse, becoming a parrot of what the lineage expects and abandoning its own knowing, will also feel and be imprinted with varying degrees of a lack of satisfaction, fulfillment and peace.

Only through the resolution of these opposites and the clearing of all judgments between parent, child and lineage can these imprints be dissolved. It is quite possible and doable, and the act of cleansing these lineage lines and expectations, hurts and disappointments can impact many millions of people immediately through the collective consciousness of the DNA of the various lineages connected to beings now alive and once alive on the planet.

The power in this situation truly resides within the latent expression of the true calling of a being. If we consider the power and energy in back of all of nature and creation, we can realize that this power is truly unlimited, eternal and all-powerful. Your personal vibrational support system is made of this power.

The Source energy can and will and does support you in making the choices which are most in alignment with your true divine purpose.

Any manner of resistance left in your field and in your thinking which would cause you to judge your family and react against them, or to kowtow to your family and give in to their desires for your expression, will simply slow the process and make it feel more difficult for you to get to what you are meant to be up to on the planet.

However, the power of life and love is so strong that it is also eternally patient, and will not become upset with you as you work through these blockages. Neither would it suggest that you become upset with yourself; rather, it will hold you in a space of love as you release judgment against yourself and others for having allowed yourself to polarize or comply.

Now it may very well be from instance to instance that the gifts of the lineage inside you are a true part of your personal dharma. It is for each one of us to know and feel into directly. Discovering and honoring the lineage gifts we are holding to whatever degree can become an important part of the healing and bridging necessary to restore peace in the consciousness, and purpose in the life and living.

Support for Your Vibration In Component 4

Allow these truth statements to wash away the residue of hindrance to showing up fully as "you" and from believing you must do as your fore parents have done, while simultaneously healing any resentment, stepping into gratitude, and helping you become fully able to reap the harvest of gifts from your lineage. Speak them out loud, or read them once a day until you feel the energies shifting.

- My true essence, vibration and inner calling is supported by the universal Source of all life.

- My true essence, vibration and inner calling are the gifts nature, life and God are offering through me to benefit all beings.

- I have the capacity to allow this true essence to emerge and be supported on this planet at this time.

- I am willing to heal through any layers of resistance, fear, compliance or rebellion I might have been experiencing in reaction against the demands of my relatives.

- I am willing to become aware of the great good gifts of my genetic and ancestral lineage and to gracefully bring them forward in divine order and in authentic ways that match the vibration of my true calling for the benefit of all.

- I am willing to allow life to guide me and to forgive my parents and their parents and so on for holding me in patterns that are not true to my personal mission.

- I am willing to be forgiven by my parents for not towing the line, for disappointing them in any way, while loving them, myself and remaining true to my inner knowing.

- Thank you Creator, God, Life, Love, for supporting me in my authentic unfolding of my natural talents and gifts so that I can participate in creation in truly aligned, joyful, productive and effective ways which serve the whole and bring me great fulfillment, satisfaction and happiness.

COMPONENT FIVE
Belief in your educational precepts which indicate a false human history, placing you within that history in an erroneous way

Let us consider the Sphinx. There are known to be hidden mysteries within it's great chambers which would reveal the vast history of your planet, far more vast than you are taught in your homes and in your schools. Even admiring the ancient statuary of the Egyptians, the Maya, the Aztecs and other ancient and considering advanced building techniques found throughout the world can hint at a more fascinating journey for humanity than we have been led to believe.

How can you expect to feel full support for your original vibration if you have been basically lied to about the larger context from which you have emerged?

Again, we are not standing in judgment of those who have hidden this knowledge from you. We are simply pointing out that you have collectively been sold a bill of goods in many ways. The layers are beginning to shed from these ancient secrets, and many of you are experiencing direct revelations of past lifetimes in cultures such as Atlantis, Lemuria and the land of Mu. Many of you are also channeling information or reading and listening to channeled information about the Galactic heritage of this planet. It is true that many star systems have contributed to life on this planet in many, many ways.

We shall discuss this more at length later in the book. In the meantime, let's focus upon the fact that you, as a vibrational being made originally with a unique signature and a specific blueprint straight from the heart of the Source of all life, have emerged into a culture and consciousness that straight out denies most of your history.

Part of you still connected always to the "Grand I Whole" of All Life, must feel subconsciously or overtly uncomfortable with this deception. It is as if you are being asked to play a game of hide and seek but part of you can see where everyone is hiding.

What is the fun of that game? Instead of pushing against the river, we usually energetically comply by agreeing with the lies and 'going along with it.'

I am aware that you can feel the residual sadness carried by yourself and other beings for having had to bare the loneliness of knowing the full truth is not being revealed while simultaneously masking this awareness from yourself so that you can exist in this dimension and function like a proper human being.

This discomfort is likely far greater than you realize. When you begin to feel again the vibrations of your true nature, the pure, unadulterated love and joy that you are, you will begin to distinguish more and more the difference between those formerly dampened vibrations and those of your essence. Truly we must have compassion for ourselves! Every ounce of hurt and suppressed feeling of betrayal for being lied to or swayed in ways against your own nature are up for healing and resolution.

The process can be as gentle as we desire, though feeling emotional energy may be part of it. Simply allow any emotions that emerge to be fully felt. In this way they will be resolved and healed.

Consider the text books written by approved sources, telling your recent histories from very particular perspectives.

Do you really think the history books contain an accurate reflection of what has happened on your planet?

Do you really believe that rote learning of these written 'facts' truly qualifies you with historical knowledge in which to accurately place yourself in context to the reality in which you currently reside? As this time of great revelation progresses, you will become increasingly astounded at the depths of the deceptions perpetrated upon humanity.

We are not saying this for you to despair however, so please understand. We are simply preparing a portalway for energetic understanding which will assist you in remaining emotionally stabilized as expanded 'truth' is revealed about exactly 'what has been going on' on your planet.

For now, the most potent and loving thing we suggest is for you to acknowledge that your earth's history, both recent and past, is far grander, more fascinating, and adventurous than anything you can at present fully imagine.

Live in the knowing of this truth. Rest and reside in the flowing and flowering of the details and overviews which will be forthcoming in perfect timing and divine order for your edification and for stimulating your memory.

Once again we remind you of the old adage, Ask And ye shall receive. This applies also to any questions you may have about the true nature of the history of earth. While you may or may not receive such answers immediately, a true and genuine asking based on a desire to heal, understand and become whole again will receive its due answer in due time.

This is truly a very exciting time for all of us as the gateways of light and information are about to be opened once again. We are wanting to pave the way to a readiness to receive and explore your history in healthy ways that will assist you in more readily understanding what your family of humankind has been through, where you are now in the grand scheme of things and where you are going.

Understanding more about your relationship to the stars and the beings on other planets, your relationship to the spiritual Source of all life, and your relationship with nature will assist you greatly in 'piecing yourself back together' so to speak. Humpty must be restored to oneness and wholeness. This will happen through the unique efforts of every single one of you.

Support for Your Vibration In Component 5: Your Historical Context

- Know that all is well even while you do not know all there is to be known about your history.

- Be willing to be as open minded as possible to the true facts of your life and existence.

- Ask to be assisted in receiving only accurate information through books, media, people or your direct source connection.

- Know and trust that you will be guided in this time of revelation to the information you need to heal and grow in the best possible sequence for you.

- Know and trust that you, your mission and your larger perspective are all part of a divine plan for the restoration of this planetary sphere.

- As you rest in this knowing without guilt, judgment, blame or shame for what has happened upon this planet in the past and what is currently happening, you will become increasingly ready to serve an awakening humanity at your highest capacity.

- Trust in the eternal now and know that all is well, that all information is contained in the holographic wholeness which exists everywhere always as All That Is, and that you are in direct communion with this wholeness at all times whether or not you are aware of it.

- Allow your vibration to be restored piece by piece as the soul fragments return to you from places they have been stuck in traumas of many lifetimes.

- Allow yourself to remember that which will serve you on your path to total awakening.

- Know that the power of love is the most potent power and it will help you through everything, even this portal of remembering.

COMPONENT SIX
Belief that you are disconnected from your Source Energy and that you do not have direct access to All That Is, all resources, all love and all light

In our fragmentation experience, or should I say experiment, we self-selected ourselves to undergo a dismantling of conscious awareness to experience a sense of separation from our oneness. Why we did this is open to many different perspectives. Let us simply acknowledge for now that this has occurred. And for whatever personal reason, we did choose to have this experience as far fetched as that may sound.

The simple acknowledgement that we chose this experience is enough to set in motion a restoration of our true vibration.

For if we are the ones who chose it and can that powerfully create an experience, surely we can now through our conscious awareness and acknowledgment of our wholeness and oneness choose again to restore ourselves.

So if we follow this thread of logic, we will realize that this belief that we are disconnected has been experienced as very real to us for many, many lifetimes.

Those of us who have been graced by the energies of faith throughout the earth's history have been lucky indeed.

For even as the prodigal son who shepherded himself away from his Father's kingdom and forgot his own heritage, blueprint and birthright, so too have we consciously or unconsciously chosen to apparently cut ourselves off from the love of the eternal Being with whom we are actually one.

Making our way back to our Father-Mother's Home which is our true domain we must make our way through the illusions that caused us to take the journey in the first place. This is where bravery, faith and love come in to assist us. For if we truly are One with the Source, do you not think this same Source would lovingly guide us back at the proper time to our true stature?

When we return from this long journey our Mother will wash our garments and our bodies, soaping us up with the divine love and wisdom which will allow us to release all the hurts and turn them into understandings of who we are and how life works.

Our Father will set us upon his knee and ask us to tell the story of our adventures so that we can integrate what has happened to us and make great good value of all of it for the benefit of the whole.

The inner sanctum sanctorum of our King-Queen-Chi-Domain is fresh and full of energy, life and beautiful gardens of consciousness. Within it we can seek and find all knowledge, heal all traumas, and understand all reflections.

This is often accounted in the near death experiences of those who go to the other side and return as messengers. We get to examine our lives and what has happened, so we can make sense out of it, grow, and come to new conclusions about more loving ways to live. Just imagine for a second being the loving Father-Mother God to whom ALL the children are returning.

Imagine the delight, the joy and the celebration as each child makes his or her own way back to their rightful heritage of their own effort. Imagine the vast information, experience, wisdom and knowledge that comes back to the King-Queendom through this process, for the benefit of all the children and the great Father-Mother God in it's acts of creation through love.

Truly now we can begin to make sense of the grand plan and orchestration which at times seems and feels so extremely nonsensical.

Many have asked and will continue to ask, "Why would a loving God allow such suffering?" And of course, for the compassionate heart, this is a powerful and necessary question on the path of awakening.

Verily we say unto you, it is not the Father-Mother God Who insisted you leave the King-Queendom of God's Divine Light.

It is the impulse of creation inside the aspects of the creator which chose to journey away into these waters. The Father-Mother God allows all, sees all, has compassion for all. Even if we choose to do things which will harm us, there is utter allowing. You may receive warnings, impulses and hints that you are about to do something which is not sanctioned by your Father-Mother God, who wants only good for you.

However, you will never be loved less for having made that choice. In fact, the celebration, joy and awakening at your return is even grander as your Divine Parents and your siblings witness your return to love.

So please open your mind if it pleases you, to understand that each of his own choosing has wrought the path of experience upon which he or she treads.

The vibrational calling card of your true nature became mixed up with vibrations of a lesser nature as you traversed different pathways, made decisions for or against your greater personal well being, and experienced eons of lifetimes. The nature of God is truly Eternal. All of your adventures are always embraced by the endless Presence of your God who loves you, who is you at your core. The backdrop and foundational reality for everything any being has ever experienced is this everlasting love and patience, witnessing, watching, awaiting your desire to return home.

There is endless assistance available to you on your return journey even as there has been on your outward adventure, though often you did not recognize it. That was all part of the adventure. And now as you have come to the completion of a cycle of the out breath of our creator, expressing as you in form, your own awareness brings you into harmony with the endless assistance that has always been there for you, so that you can access it and leverage it as often and robustly as you choose.

Truly stilling the heart, mind and soul is the way in, the way to receptivity of this Guidance.

You will be able to navigate back through endless layers of confusing it by simply quieting your mind and body and listening deeply. Connecting to your Mother planet which houses your body and nourishes it will also assist you in experiencing even more joy and health than you can imagine. She is there for you just as your Father-Mother God in Heaven is always there for you.

Support for Your Vibration In Component 6

- Be still and know that you are God.

- The Kingdom of Heaven is within you.

- I and my Father-Mother God are One.

- Love the Lord thy God with all thy strength, all thy might and all thy soul, and all else will be added unto you.

- Worry not for what you will eat or drink.

- Cleave unto Me.

- Feel the love that we are together in your heart as very real and substantial. As simple as that sounds, it is extremely profound and can cause an immediate shift in the results of your life.

COMPONENT SEVEN
Emotional Trauma Caused by the Embedding of All Components Over Time, and In Your Genetic Lineages

As we explore the components which have woven together to variously muddle and hide your true vibrational signature, we begin to get a picture of the nature of the mess we are cleaning up. Without such a perspective it is easy to simply feel overwhelmed, scared or depressed without fully understanding why.

Breaking these components down into bite sized bits helps us to reflect upon the distinction between your original unhampered, untouched, untarnished vibration and the illusions which have crisscrossed their way into your energy field as transparent overlaid images change the base image when all are simultaneously projected on a wall. The base image is still there, it is just harder to see it until the many layers are removed.

In perfect timing and divine order, we begin to access the tools which will remove these false images piece by piece by piece, until our fields are clear again and we know-sense-feel and remember who we are.

Imagine that there are two primary types of transparencies which need to be dealt with. One are the overlays projected on you by your parents, family, and genetic lineage. The other are the overlays from the traumas of other lifetimes. Additional types of overlays include the cultural beliefs and patternings of the day, the projections made upon you by your friends, associates and communities, and influences from what are known as parallel life times or alternate probability lines. Needless to say, it is easy to understand how an individual can become confused and a vibration muddled through such a series of events. Breaking down the imagery like this, we can see though that the clean up process is manageable.

How can we assist this process in accelerating? The Light and Love that you are shining from deep within you, simply dissolves away those false transparencies over time. We offer two techniques to allow this Light and Love to do It's mighty work: The Pink Light of Unconditional Love, and Core Star Activation.

These two techniques are ways of leveraging the ever-present "first step" of 'cleaving unto God' or Love. Here are some practical ways for getting into the state of loving God with all your heart, strength and mind. These acts keep you in the higher vibrations while the unwanted vibrations sort themselves out.

The Pink Light of Unconditional Love

Imagine a beautiful pink iridescent light shimmering above, below and all around about you. Especially do this when you are feeling less than fully whole, good or worthy, or when another person is bothering you in any way. Consistency over time is the key here. Make it a habit. With your inner eye, imagine yourself as a happy, smiling little child, bathed in this beautiful light of pure unconditional love. You can also imagine this pink light bathing others with whom you are interacting, and imagine them as an innocent, smiling child, to help soothe uncomfortable situations.

Core Star Activation

Core Star Activation is a process of attuning and aligning deeply with Source Creator within your very own heart. Through this alignment process, with the expansion of the very Light-Love of the Creator itself within you, it becomes easy to see the patterns and energetics that are still floating in your aura and body-mind. See Resources Section for information on learning Core Star Activation and for supporting materials.

Actions To Accelerate Healing

Make these actions a habit to accelerate your healing and alignment process:

- The Light of God surrounds me, the Love of God enfolds me, the Power of God protects me, and the Presence of God watches over me. Wherever I AM, God IS and all is well. (Unity Prayer)

- When you are speaking with people, especially if you find yourself in a hurry, repeat with your inner voice I love you, I love you, I love you, as you listen to what they have to say. This will help you focus upon the moment, hear them, and will help them also to feel at peace while they express to you.

As we are able to interact with seers and healing facilitators who can help us identify and clear individual layers, and as we come more into our own unified field consciousness and can see and clear these layers ourselves, the pile will become less and less dense.

Leverage the Power of Affirmations. When you are doing affirmations from a place of clarity, and also clearing the remnants of the false beliefs contrary to the affirmations, these can be a great tool for realignment and recalibrating your vibration. We recommend sitting in the morning and stating these affirmations out loud. You can also print them out and place them somewhere that you can see each day.

7 Affirmations for Returning To Truth

The Truth of your Being is pure, divine innocence, oneness with All That Is, and eternal love. Allow these 7 Affirmations to help you return to the realization of the truth of who you are.

Affirmation for Component 1
I am pure, innocent and good.

Affirmation for Component 2
I am abundantly blessed and supplied

Affirmation for Component 3
I am a free being, an extension of the Source Prime Creator in Form. My life is my own. I am free, I am free, I am free.

Affirmation for Component 4
I am my own unique expression of Life Itself. My mind, heart and circumstances allow me to fully express what I came here for in total peace with all those around me.

Affirmation for Component 5
I now open to receive insight and knowledge around my true origins and the true history of earth. I am now willing to see through illusion.

Affirmation for Component 6
I am At One with my Creator, Pure Divine Source. I now have and have always had direct access to All That Is, all resources, all love and all light.

Affirmation for Component 7

I now ASK Prime Creator to dissolve all trauma lines from these components over time, easily, gently, gracefully, harmoniously, and in peace.

Eventually logic dictates we will certainly be left with only the pure base pattern of our original core vibration. With our clarity and divine remembrance restored, a whole new type of adventure is upon us. From this state we can begin to assist others simply by our very presence in extremely profound ways. We will be the empty channel, the glass and what fills the glass all at once—witnessing, observing, allowing, and loving all.

LISTENING TO THE INNER VOICE: STARSEED TECHNOLOGIES

We are the Star Elders of the Council of Mu. We are the ones who were here when the world itself was one, when the continents were in fact as one body of land and when the consciousness of love, peace and harmony were erect on this planet. From our love and our witnessing, we are sharing this message to assist you on your journey home.

We are recognizing the deep interstellar nature of our communion as we have progressed on to embody our beings in various star systems and on myriad planets in the many galaxies of creation.

Even so we are innately and intrinsically one with you. There is no separation. This idea of us and them, aliens and natives, is as illusory as the fragmented mind which allows some to be fed and cared for on your planet and others, not.

The restoration of a true cosmic consciousness is what we are about, and we seek to interact with you our relatives in nurturing, uplifting and helpful ways to bring in this new era on your beautiful planet we once called home.

There is no need to fear, though many may and many will as the awareness that humanity is not a singular race in creation becomes acutely realized.

There will be more activity in the upcoming months and years as you all come into harmony with your connections with your star ancestors. Your star ancestors are here at the beckoning and call for help from many earth beings who have suffered enough.

We do carry many gifts and realizations for you, and mostly we are here to hold space, to witness your process, and to love you through it. You see we are more connected than you at this current moment to our awareness of universal resourcefulness and total divine order.

There are many star beings on many levels in many galaxies and multiple universes. There are also therefore many levels of awareness and unwinding even among the star beings.

You will always know you are on track and in communion with beings who are in alignment with your highest good if love, light and happiness are the keynote of your feeling and intuition. We are not here to push any agenda, to make anything happen, or to force you in any way.

Quite to the contrary, we are available at your bidding to assist you in awakening to your own true inner power and potential.

This is our only calling. Many of you have heard of galactic law and the governance systems and principles of noninterference. We do abide by these principles; however, it is a little different in feeling nature than how you would typically tend to interpret it from your current perspective.

It is not a rule based reality as yours is at this time. There is an inner harmony and resonance with the collective realization that we are witnessing, holding space and allowing you to grow and heal at your own pace.

There is an agreement through love that we do not assist without being asked and that we do not take action without being invited. This is simply a natural essence of our being which exists for us as we connect to the All That Is through the love that we are. Do you see the difference?

A Galactic Federation with noninterference rules feels very strong, hard and rule based just like your systems whereas the reality we are coming from exists through resonance with what is truly the highest and best for all beings.

We exist and operate through The Field and therefore our Source Connection guides us collectively and individually to actions that are love based and whole.

As we are recognizing that you indeed are our relatives, and that you indeed also have the power and presence of Love within you, we have the deepest respect for you and see you as true equals.

We are not coming to save you or to control you or to modify you, simply we are here because our hearts call us to be in attendance as you go through your growing pains just as we have gone through in the past. As we all progress on the path back home to God, to Oneness, to full realization, we have great compassion because we have experienced what you are experiencing now.

Does this make sense?

This is a subtle yet important distinction which will help you make a step toward understanding the distinction between a dualistic reality and a oneness based experience.

This important subtlety shall give you the needed clues to guide your own actions into a higher octave for truly you can't get here from there, you can't change a system from within the created system.

It is necessary to see things from a different perspective in order to do things differently and therefore get different results.

We truly do love and appreciate you for being here on the earth plane at this time and for suffering so many injustices in the name of love, We are standing with you as we know love will prevail and you will be set free by the innermost essence of your own being, true love.

This inner reconnection with the divine heart of true love is available to each of us. It is the place within us that comforts, soothes, knows all, feels all and knows what the next right action step is, always. There are many ways to reconnect yourself to this divine light and love within. This frequency of love has the capacity to melt away fear and to establish new vibrations which can cause great healings to take place. The true essence of true love exists within you right now even if you cannot see it or feel it. Accessing this gateway is the single most important thing you can do for yourself now.

Through the power and presence of true love your so-called miracles take place. We would call these not miraculous but normal expected experiences for all beings who are residing in love. Love's great magnetic and attractive power will always bring good where good has been sown.

It is the veritable law of life. As we come into harmony with this law of life we will experience ever increasing instances of what we call synchronicity, miracles, and just simple joy.

There are many specifics embedded within this overarching topic of what we call Love's Great Doorway. As we move into this material we will become more specific with you to offer ideas which might assist you in achieving greater access to your own personal miracle matrix.

Your heart center is a gateway into the infinite portals of creation. Through it you can reconnect with all beings and heal all things. This is the love manufacturing center which is Causative in the ultimate sense. In the great disturbances of your planet wherein there has been a separation, in consciousness and experience between you and your Source, between one another and between you and nature, this has manifested most profoundly as a separation between head and heart.

The great reconnection has to do with remedying this disconnectedness and reestablishing the Kingdom-Queendom (Chi Domain) of Heaven within you.

As you reside in the heart center and operate from that space of love, and as you allow the mind to be the servant of the heart, you are operating through the unified field of consciousness which contains and is all things, all beings, all timelines, all knowledge, all wisdom, all light and all love.

As you reside within that heart space as the center of your consciousness, you have access not only to data and information for yourself and others but also to the love and compassion that is necessary for any kind of healing and restoration to occur. It is more commonly felt in your human males that there is a definite feeling of separation between the head and the heart. Repairing this matrix of connection is what we are about at this time through many lightworkers who are busily attending to an awakening humanity.

The manner and method of restoring this heart-mind connection is really quite simple. If you realize that your entire physical and energetic / spiritual / emotional bodies are woven together with energy lines, you will realize that the reparation of these energy lines is the way to heal the connection between head and heart. Different types of disconnected thought forms build upon one another over time, through generations and end up as an experience of true disconnection.

To repair this, we simply move into the heart chakra area with our consciousness, and allow the energies and warmth there to grow into a blazing sun.

Energy and manifestation follow attention. This is why all that is necessary is for us to put our attention upon the heart chakra of an individual with an intent for it to open, flourish and grow in warmth and light.

As this heart chakra reignites the energy flow, you can allow the flame like light to burn away the dross of the past. Misconceptions, old hurts, wounds and encrusted experience residues begin to melt away. A simple act of bringing the focus and awareness back into the heart center will begin to retrain the mind to become once again the rightful servant to the heart.

A successful practitioner will be able to feel and/or see the energy of a person who is operating from the head. The energies of annoyance, confusion, lack of clarity and even blame, shame or guilt can only emerge from the mind.

These symptoms of expression also offer clues as one is witnessing oneself or another on the cusp of awakening.

So the trusty guide simply witnesses that this is what is occurring.

And since this guide level person is also witnessing the truth of the divine nature of the person and holding space for the natural release of that which is not natural, the practitioner finds it easier and easier to reside in a state of non-attached awareness and unconditional love which are prerequisites for the true healing path.

This state of unconditional love and non-attached awareness allows the person being assisted to feel honored, whole, accepted and at peace even while they are being instructed. The egoless ego of the practitioner has no agenda other than to assist where called, therefore, there is no resistance as the ego mechanics of the individual being assisted are witnessed.

The path of life itself is the temple and cauldron through which the initiate must pass in order to become of this level of service. Dedication, time, commitment and relaxed awareness are hallmarks of such a practitioner. You can recognize the presence of such a being by the way you feel. If you feel whole, complete and accepted even in your apparent state of disconnection, you are likely in the presence of such a one. We can all learn how to attain and maintain these states. It is part of our divine nature and rightful heritage to reclaim.

As we each further and further embrace the path of love and healing, we become the witness more and more. There is an ongoing willingness toward self examination as we repair our thinking and allow love to 'correct' that which has been twisted, like a spinal adjustment of the mind and heart.

This correction is an other than perfect word as to our typical thinking it might imply something was 'wrong' before it was corrected. This is the very wounding of the separation itself.

We come to realize that as the ego begins to heal, it may be quite sensitive to any words that ping on the idea of it being wrong, disabled, inappropriate, bad or damaged.

The ego personality as the instrument of the separated mind can begin to return to alignment with it's larger self.

As it does so, we as practitioners learn to hold space for this healing with a great level of awareness as to the specific insults that have been perpetrated upon each person or egoic nature.

These specific insults result in testy areas where the person might bite back or become depressed if the words hit them wrong.

This is why we train to become highly aware of the words we speak and the energies carried behind them, striving always to live and speak with the greatest possible extension of respect, love and regard for the feelings of another. In this way, space is held for an eventual restoration of the ego personality to wholeness.

These simple methods take practice and we encourage you to begin where you are. There is no hurry on the path to awakening yet there certainly is a feeling of urgency. Instead of worrying about this feeling of urgency, simply dedicate yourself to taking the necessary action steps to progress yourself most profoundly and joyfully on your path. The feeling of urgency is there for many reasons, including the time sequence which you are currently in, which has so much emphasis on an 'end of the world' scenario. These pressures in the back of the consciousness can show up as stress, tension or worry, or even depression.

Because you have experienced feeling disconnected from your Source, you have also experienced a less than full, solid connection with your intuition and inner guidance.

This too has led to further self-doubt, fear and anxiety which, though it may seem subtle or buried, is actually a big pressure on the minds and hearts of many beings.

We cannot beseech you enough to be gentle with yourselves. It is the energy of the separation which would chastise, punish or rebuke you for being disconnected. Do you see? The wound self-perpetuates and grows worse as we continue to beat up on ourselves for seeming to be less than perfect. Mercy and grace prevail.

First and foremost, we must have mercy upon ourselves. We must extend this mercy, grace and unconditional forgiveness upon ourselves. If a child lost it's way in the woods and got hurt, would love really be mad at it as it found it's way back home? Of course not. We must learn to be that love to ourselves.

In this way, we begin to throw off the trappings of insanity which would punish us further for being wounded. Often those closest to us in our lives will exhibit this same kind of behavior. They might not know to extend love to us or to themselves — as they may not even be aware that they or you have accrued wounds of a mental-emotional-spiritual and sometimes physical nature through these lifetimes of experience.

As we become stronger through loving ourselves and being gentle with ourselves, it will become easier for us to relinquish the need to take in others' criticism or rebukes.

We will begin to see them as wounded, for whenever someone is chastising or rebuking another, from our perspective, that being is acting out of a wounded place. From this new vantage point of realization, you can begin to practice the various techniques which will assist you in rebalancing yourself in relation to that person, and possibly, if called, even be a source of light in their life.

Some people seem to stubbornly resist the light and love we shine upon them. We say to you, this is okay. Keep shining, yet remove all attachment to outcome. Cease to worry for whether or not they will ever change. Perhaps they will, perhaps they won't. Simply shine upon them from close or from afar, knowing all is well.

Unconditionally accept that they are where they are where they are. This is what is at this moment, and there are reasons why it is so. Have compassion for the person and for the reasons, the many many reasons, which have brought them to this current state of disconnect.

In this way, in this cauldron of total acceptance, miracles do eventually occur. It is also a relief to you because you realize you no longer need to attempt to fix, change or alter them in any way.

Simply extend love to them, and know that all is well. Your increasing psychic and spiritual guidance and awareness will show you the way in your relations with them. Follow that guidance through love and with a forgiving heart and you will discover that you are liberated from the tangled web that once bound you to a painful way of being with that person.

We are wanting to express to you how very grateful we are for the time and patience it takes to open yourselves to the higher energies. We realize fully the complex nature of your earth life interactions, the love that you have carried through so many challenges, and the desire of your heart to be free, to express, to share and to aspire. We sand in support of your individual and collective transformation as you choose to release the past and all its imprints so that you can move from the constrictions of a separation consciousness into life from the resonant field.

TOOLS OF THE DECEPTION

When we refer to the deception, we are speaking about the subtle or not so subtle mechanisms which keep the separation consciousness firmly in place.

The energies which have become accustomed to this fragmented way of being and which have been leveraging its many aspects to its own disconnected personal advantage do not necessarily want the healing that many are calling for at this time.

This does not mean they will not eventually want it for they will, in their own time and in their own way. Also sometimes these deceptions are not embodied in a person as much as they are embodied in a collective consciousness thought field.

There are many cultural conceptions taken as truth which need to be reexamined from the point of view of love and understanding. The energies of Grace provide us with ways and means to accomplish this tricky task.

What does love do? What does fear do?

Merely asking ourselves this question when faced with some kind of discomfort will help us to 'break it down' and leverage the power of wisdom.

LOVE

- Love accepts and sees things as they are.

- Love understands there is a vast history which has resulted in making things and people the way they are.

- Love understands that at the core, all beings have come from love and deserve love, no matter what.

- Love understands that created beings have been through a very intense experience which has caused many fractures in consciousness and many wounds: physically, mentally, emotionally and spiritually.

- Love understands that at the core, all beings, no matter how seemingly bad they are, desire to be understood, accepted and to share their gifts.

- Love understands that all beings have been frustrated to some degree in experiencing these basic desires, and that this has left an intrinsic sadness within them to varying degrees.

- Love therefore knows that in every encounter, there is a potential for tenderness, acceptance and healing that far surpasses any judgments we might make from our worldly perspective about how a person is showing up.

- Love understands the repercussions of actions from a past life timeline and a genetic lineage inheritance perspective have taken their toll on everyone, and that these are the factors which are causative to the way everyone is showing up at this time. Therefore love has compassion for the suffering of all beings and can extend that unconditionally to them in an unwavering manner.

- Love embraces all, feels all, recognizes all and allows all.

- Love desires for their to be resolution, peace, forgiveness and healing in every instance.

- Love places the ego personality in it's right relationship with the Universal divine consciousness and places the heart as parent and guide to the mind.

- Love works from within a Unified Resonant Field which includes yet transcends all polarities.

- Love seeks to authentically offer helpful solutions to make things better.

FEAR

- Fear judges, labels, and makes things right, wrong, good or bad.

- Fear is quick to react and slow to listen.

- Fear asks us to cut ourselves off from others and to think they will harm us.

- Fear supports our belief in our own ego's dominion over reality.

- Fear tells us to run, hide, blame, shame and resent.

- Fear has an emotional component which we can feel as a negative energy.

- Fear asks us to project our own inner disfunction onto others.

- Fear suggests there is no hope.

- Fear seeks to control situations in order to feel safe.

- Fear imposes its own will instead of seeing clearly that each unique being is a sovereign being and has a right to its own perspective.

- Fear imprisons love, while love releases fear.

- Fear compares for its own advantage and wants to compartmentalize people, places and things to feel safe.

- Fear tends to think in black and white.

The acts of the separation mentality can sometimes be very subtle and tricky to discern.

Often separation consciousness will disguise itself as love and light. You will feel something is off yet you may in the past not have been able to break down the problem into bite sized bits. What makes this type of scenario even more tricky, is that the person or people who are bringing falsehood forward as truth may be doing so subconsciously.

They may not be, and are likely not, aware of their own ego control game. They will be attempting to convince you in a subtle or overt way to adopt their perspective, and they will truly believe they are correct.

- For those of you who are more open, receptive and accepting, and for those of you who seek approval of others, it may feel difficult to speak your truth that something is off because you don't want to hurt their feelings, you don't want them to get mad at you, or you don't want to appear to be rude.

- For those of you who have no trouble overtly stating your opinion, if you do so with any type of resistance, resentment, judgment or anger, the person then may feel they have a 'reason' to lash out at you or make you wrong in some way.

To know one's own personality tendencies during these subtle interactions is very helpful.

Whether one is more the 'nice guy,' or more of the confronter type, one needs to learn how to pause, witness and accept that something is off.

Continue to listen while you track the information coming through. Resist the temptation to react or respond immediately. Open yourself to the Unified Field of all consciousness which knows and sees all, and become curious. Why am I feeling something is off? What is the specific thing that does not feel right to me, even though so much of what they are saying appears accurate or strong?

How can I help myself to grow stronger while helping this person to see through any illusion they may be carrying, successfully, without damaging the relationship? This kind of asking and openness to the Unified Field will help you step by step to be able to sort through the tricky bits of your interactions. Remember, your goal, if you desire to be a harbinger of love's truest teachings, is not to make the other person wrong, be right, come out on top, or slay the evil dragon.

Your role is to see clearly, to hold a space of unconditionality and non-judgment which allows all concerned to learn, aspire and grow stronger. The separation consciousness would judge, blame and cast away such a person or conversation.

The love consciousness would seek a higher octave of togetherness and healing which can emerge through our open willingness to really listen:

a) to the other person,
b) to our own feelings and insights and discernments, and

c) to the universal information streaming to us from the Unified Field, which is always available if we ask.

The time is approaching where more and more of you will be able to accurately discern between these subtleties and hold a space of love to assist others in seeing the distinction. For even the most hardened of controlling beings who have delighted in fear based thinking are now often open to learning and growing and changing.

If we do not judge them, we have an opportunity to get through to them. If we can learn to speak to them with love, humility, and wisdom, the sharp sword of our discernment has a chance to get through to them, and strengthen our own inner acceptance of our own correct insights.

The fact is, you have enough information to be able to discern at this point whether something comes from love or it does not. Whether you totally trust your instincts or not is another question. Part of the task of spiritual evolution is to become willing to pay attention and give credence to the inner signals, imagery and feelings you are receiving.

CORRECTING SPIRITUAL MISPERCEPTIONS

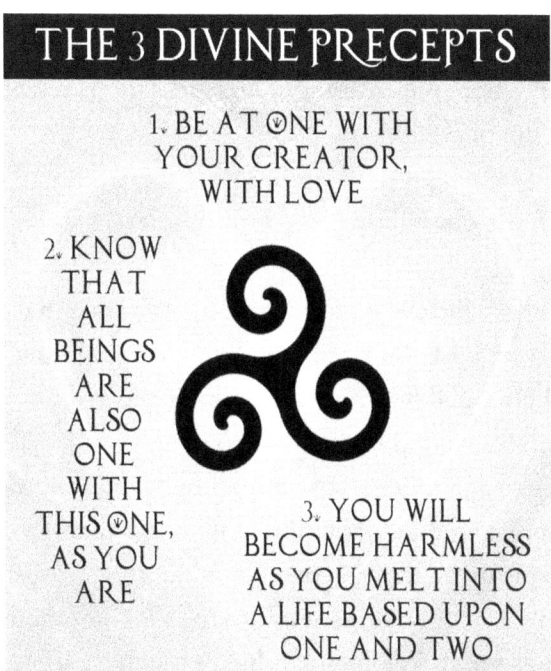

THE 3 DIVINE PRECEPTS

1. BE AT ONE WITH YOUR CREATOR, WITH LOVE

2. KNOW THAT ALL BEINGS ARE ALSO ONE WITH THIS ONE, AS YOU ARE

3. YOU WILL BECOME HARMLESS AS YOU MELT INTO A LIFE BASED UPON ONE AND TWO

We are fascinated as we witness the many pulses and changes in conscious awareness on your planet.

There are so many misconceptions layered upon misconceptions when it comes to things of a spiritual nature. Truly the grand and great spiritual teachings many of which have come through your religious systems, have been muddied, stepped on, twisted, misused and sullied by those who have either been attempting to control you or those who have bought into the control and are trying to do good by spreading what is actually falsehood. Since this pattern has been playing out for many centuries, we realize the profound nature of the confusion that can occur when one attempts to sort out the cherries from the pits.

One finds oneself with a couple choices:

1. Either attempt to sort out the original core essence of the teachings of a great religion from the available fragments which have likely been mistranslated to some degree; or
2. Throw out religion altogether and attempt to access the information you need directly from your own Source; or
3. What most beings tend to do is a combination of these two. We have all likely received some kind of insight from a phrase or saying from a great religious precept. We know there is universal truth living within these master teachings. Yet if we have not eyes to see and ears to hear, we run the risk of perpetuating the same mistranslations that have caused so much havoc to begin with.

When we examine the core, basic teachings of all the traditions, there are many universal truths which can be deciphered. When these in fact resonate with your own inner sounding board connected to a love-based perception of reality, you can know you are on the right track. What are the Core Spiritual Teachings? We are going to count them as three in number to begin this conversation.

The Three Divine Precepts[3]

1. Be At One with your Creator, with Love.
2. Know that all beings are also one with this One, as you are.
3. You will become harmless as you melt into a life based upon one and two.

Let's examine precepts 1, 2 and 3 from several points of view to come into a higher resonant understanding of where we have been and where we are going in a spiritual sense.

PRECEPT 1:
BE AT ONE WITH YOUR CREATOR, WITH LOVE

If we have been wounded by religion and its uncanny methods of control and manipulation, we

---

[3] [3] See glossary of terms for explanation of the use of "Precept"

may be in a state of reaction against the use of the word God, thinking it is indicating a bipolar Father figure who alternately loves and adores us, then hates and punishes us.

The schisms this belief system has created are very deep and can begin to heal through correcting the perception and understanding where the direct falsehoods lie. If we have been trained to embrace religious dogma, there may be fear involved in our relationship with our perceived God, and it is likely this God is believed to be outside of ourselves, looking down upon us, and judging us.

Nothing could be further from the truth.

There are beings (you might call them fallen angels or advanced souls) whom scriptures indicate when speaking of personalities. Any time you are hearing or seeing a reference to a God who seeks to punish you in any way, or who seeks to control or manipulate your behavior, you can rest assured you are hearing about one of these beings.

All beings are on a trajectory of awakening, even the so called more advanced beings. None are immune to the call of personal alchemical transmutation, for all of us are in this universal pot of life, this veritable endless sea of consciousness, together. If we can begin to comprehend that the Gods of our religions may be indicating personalities who were more powerful than the people they 'ruled over,' we can begin to sort out the mythologies from the facts.

The one called Jesus came to shift us from a fear-based mythological religion to a practice of Universal Divine Love, with a direct connection to that Source of Love we call God.

Many are the messengers of this love. They have existed throughout all time and in all cultures. Consider Rumi, Tabir and Hafiz, the ancient Sufi mystic poets, who relentlessly inspire us to rekindle that direct connection with Pure Love.

Consider Buddha who said, "I relinquish all teachers and all teachings," and who went on to stubbornly sit under the Bodhi tree until he reached enlightenment — the sealing of Light within the consciousness of his vessel.

The divine universal principles of non-attachment, desirelessness and centered, balanced living were brought forth and variously interpreted by people who then made a religion from his teachings, following one who relinquished all teachers and 'went direct.'

We say this with all due respect to aspirants from every religion, with a total and complete understanding that all aspirants are and have been doing their best on the path to awakening throughout all time. Now, we simply wish to offer that if you are to actually emulate your great spiritual masters and what they did, this might be a very different practice than tacitly following rules written in a book by people of the past who interpreted these teachers' actions and decided what people should do to follow or worse, worship them.

We say 'worse' in this context because it can become a tool of the separation. In other words, of course every tenet is a double-edged sword, and when one worships Jesus or Buddha as God, cleaving unto them and coming in unto them spiritually with every fiber of your being, there can be of course great progress made, as through the ancient guru-disciple practice.

However, if one worships another being as God without realizing that that One is also the same as you, a Being of God, then further separation can be created. Our point of our spiritual practice is to unify ourselves once again with that effervescent, all seeing, all knowing, all powerful, all loving Being that is the One Being behind the Many, dancing as each of us in this illusory world of form for the sheer fun, joy, adventure of it. Even Jesus said, "Ye are Gods," and "The Kingdom of Heaven is within YOU."

So again, let us indicate that Love is always aware of context and can discern these things, situation by situation.

The act of cleaving unto God, loving God, becoming one with God and the thought about it are two different things. Simply following rote methodology passed on through hierarchy and ritual where the core purpose of the ritual was forgotten is not the same as actually living this principle in daily life.

If you are someone who has come to hate the idea of God because you see through the thin veil of religious fallacy, then the idea of clinging to, loving or becoming one with such a God might feel nauseating. For you, we wish to indicate that God is Universal Principle, beyond all religion, beyond all ritual, beyond all sanctioned behavior patterning in the physical reality. The God of Universal Principle, the Prime Creator which created all beings and all things through an act of Love, does not care what you call it. It merely awaits your readiness and desire to reconnect with it in your own unique way, as you wish, when you wish, how you wish.

Any act of love or kindness reconnects you to this Consciousness. Every desire to aspire has in it the seeds of love of God / Creator / Source.

There is no right or wrong way; however, there are guideposts for the true aspirant. To love God, therefore, with all your heart, strength and mind might also translate as, fall in love with LOVE, fall in love with LIFE, remind yourself daily and moment by moment that LOVE is the grandest power which will set you free. Become one with LOVE by allowing it to flow to you and through you, by you, as you, through the center of your heart, irradiating all around you with it's precious golden light and warmth.

Become a conduit of this love from your current context and perspective. As we do these types of things increasingly, we become more and more aware of ourselves as One with this pure divine Love. This is what it means to Love God with all your being.

The idea of surrender can also be misinterpreted. "I will to will thy will."

This is not the will of an outside being who seeks to control you. This is the presence and power of the great I AM that WE ARE together, and as we align our little will of our personality – (falsely identified as separate and alone in the world because of the separation we have been experiencing) — with the will of the Grand I Whole of our One Being, then the Unified Resonant Field connection is established in us and through us. More spiritual mojo and cosmic juice can come to the planet through us, and we have access to wisdom impulses from that ENTIRE consciousness which will surely guide us to the greatest benevolence in all our acts.

Surrendering is neither a subjugation nor a failure. The ego personality, from its limited perspective, may feel that it is one of the two, or both. We can see a beautiful perfection even in the seemingly less than perfect way that religious understanding has rolled out as we witness that inner flame helping the ego personality to 'submit' to the will of God despite it's misunderstanding.

Little by little, the ever-present power of Love will work on the person who has thus relinquished control of the ego mind, and eventually this being will come to know that God is pure Love and has only the great good will of Love as its ground of being. Love wills all goodness, and love allows ALL experience. The chooser is free to choose to stay in harmony with love or to stray. As we have strayed and have suffered enough from that choice, eventually we all choose to return to love.

Religious establishments still ruled more by fear than love may feel threatened by these teachings. When an institution becomes attached to its own existence and desires it to perpetuate regardless of whether it is in its destiny to continue, we can see that it is a fear based institution. Being in the grand flow and trust of pure love and joy, an institution can change and grow along with its students.

Seeking to hold a reign of power over others, to keep them coming back, many religious institutions instill erroneous concepts of the fear of God. This self-seeking and self-serving mechanism has deep roots in the separation consciousness. We must bear witness to this fact and become discerning regarding the actual state of development of an institution and it's subscribers. There may come junctures where it is appropriate to leave one institution for a community that has grown more in the truth of this awareness.

The fear of financial loss if people grow spiritually is quite prevalent and is an age-old mechanism for attempting to keep things the same. There are many newer institutions which have more fully embraced the love principle, such as the churches of the New Thought Movement. For those who are evolving past the fear based mechanisms of more traditional churches, these may be a good next step. Some people really thrive with community, and we encourage you to find communities that truly match or exceed your own level of consciousness so that you can continue to aspire.

If your institution shows signs of holding you back, projecting fear of any kind, or not growing with you, we hold space for the choice to be made to shift, to flow, to move. The ocean of Life and Love is flowing and moving. Let's consider the energy of a spiral galaxy, the movement of waters in an ocean and the whispering of wind through trees. Over time, volcanoes, earthquakes and other events change even the land masses themselves which for periods of time seem so immovable.

If we are to be like God, to cleave unto God and to embody the principles of Love, we will also watch and look to God's Creation, the natural world, in order to grow and aspire. We will learn to flow with changes, and to release fear of these changes.

For even as death is a doorway into a new level of consciousness, so the changing of our institutions to something more useful should be embraced as a collective knowing. This puts us squarely in the place of trusting that all our needs will be met, at all times.

"Fear not for what ye shall eat or drink" applies as much to these institutions as it does to the individuals who attend them. We are all in this sea of God together, and if we are to aspire, we must flow, we must change, we must grow. Surrendering then becomes merely an act of allowing the flow of life to have its way with us.

If we can begin to identify WITH and AS this flow, surely it will not seem as scary or dangerous as if we perceive ourselves to be an outside entity being worked on by change. Loving God is to identify with God, the almighty presence that constantly moves, dances, changes, and loves in the eternal now.

Examine the following statements in the new context of what has been discussed in Precept 1:

- Love the Lord thy God with all thy heart, all thy strength and all thy might
- Cleave Unto God
- Be Love
- Surrender to God / Let Source Lead (Allow your true self that knows all, is everywhere present, and is all powerful to take the lead by placing your awareness upon this Source Within)
- I will to will Thy will
- My will and the Creator's Will are One

**PRECEPT 2:
KNOW THAT ALL BEINGS ARE ALSO
ONE WITH THIS ONE, AS YOU ARE**

When we look out at the world from our eyes, we see many beings, many things, many places, many animals, insects, trees and situations. From a consciousness of identity with our personality which seems quite limited and which has not access to the Universal mind in a conscious way, we can feel "at the effect of" all of these separate things.

We might feel that God is watching us, judging us, checking to see if we are behaving correctly, which may cause us to also look out at others to see if they are following the rules as we perceive them, or not. Often, many of us will become quite angry if others do not follow the rules we perceive to be correct. This can be quite plainly understood, forgiven and accepted as we reach an awareness in our consciousness that this anger stems from a genuine desire to 'do the right thing.'

The wound of separation has caused us to feel as if we are basically bad, wrong or unacceptable to some degree or another as discussed in our components section. Thus understood, we can begin to have compassion for ourselves, because surely, once again, at the heart of this misperception is a genuine desire to be in harmony with life. So let us forgive ourselves and all others who might look out at the world in this manner, and let us seek to truly understand the root cause of someone's anger instead of simply reacting against it.

We will react against it in our own anger if their misperception hits on one of our core wounds, causing an emotional reaction. Let us know that if we have an emotional charge ourselves, it is clear we have touched one of our core wounds, and should address this wound inside ourselves, which is the ONLY place it can truly be healed.

Technique for Overcoming Projection When Experiencing An Emotional Charge

When you notice you are experiencing an emotional charge of any kind, become aware that no matter what, there is inner work for you to do around this issue. Regardless of how "right" you feel or know you are in the situation, if you do have a charge, there is some energy to be "discharged" and a fuller realization of your Self to be retrieved.

Acknowledging the charge is the first step in retrieving the trapped energy and the part of ourselves we have judged or cast aside.

It can be helpful to "speak this discernment" to others. In other words, simply stating "I am experiencing an emotional charge," or "for some reason, I now feel angry" can help to place the dynamic into a more balanced state, because you have "taken ownership" of what you are experiencing and you are "holding back" from projecting it on the other person to the best of your ability in that moment.

Depending on the nature of the charge and its deep origins, this can be a quick and easy process or a durable and challenging one. Either way, if we realize that truth is truth, and "if I have an emotional charge there is something to heal within myself" is the bottom line from which we operate, we can no longer run or hide from the wound and give ourselves permission to get to the bottom of it. Resolve to "stick with it" until it is resolved.

1. Find the origin of the most extreme feeling of charge in your physical body. Where do you feel it? In your heart? Your liver? Is it in your whole aura or mental body? Locate the charge and the associated feelings to the best of your ability.

2. Imagine you are a tiny "you" and dive into this place of the greatest intensity. Allow yourself to "feel" and "follow the lines of" this charge wherever it takes you. This may take 20 minutes or more, or less, depending on how deep it is. Simply follow the energy, notice what you are thinking and feeling, and be reflective if images or understandings from past experiences arise. This may be in the form of the past of this lifetime or other lifetimes.

3. Harvest the wisdom gained in understanding "how" and "what" you decided about yourself or others that caused the original charge. Reflect deeply on your experience (without wallowing).

4. As you do this and emerge from the exercise, you can "check" to see if the charge is resolved

and therefore the pattern cleared, by imagining the issue that originated the experience of feeling an emotional charge as if it's happening now. Is there still a charge? If so, dive back in and keep at it until you get to the root with your LOVE, your consciousness and awareness.

5. If the charge is gone, congratulations! Now you should be better equipped to "deal with" the issues brought up in this interaction in positive and helpful ways beyond blame and shame.

If you get stuck and need help with this process, see the HELP section in the appendix.

Alternatively, practices such as EFT (Emotional Freedom Technique) and many other modalities can also help dissolve such charges. Or, you can simply do a basic Source Alignment Process.

EXERCISE: Source Alignment Process

1. Tune in to the center of your heart.
2. Simply quiet your mind and breathe from your heart.
3. Ask your Creator, God, Love to clear for you whatever energies or issues are coming up for you now.

4. Witness the clearing take place in whatever way you 'see,' feel or know in your mind's eye.
5. Wait on the inner confirmation and give thanks for the clearing.

In this self reflective manner, we can also begin to hold space for others, even if they have not reached this stage yet of perception which allows them to self reflect on their own wounds. Only through holding the field of love and acceptance of what is, with a core intention for clarity and healing to emerge, can we hope to assist them in clearing up misunderstandings that cause them to project and become angry when others aren't following their 'rules'. This practice takes a dedicated awareness which grows day by day when we intend it to. Simply make a request of some nature to your own inner being, for clarity, grace, mercy and understanding to emerge more and more each day, in your own being and in all interactions with all others.

In this way the strong arm of compassion embraces us and holds us up, as the light dawns in our consciousness and we begin to recognize that the others around us are just like us. Not only do they suffer from the same core wounds, but they also spring from the same divine Love and seek to return to it.

All of their actions whether helpful, rebellious, naughty, nice or mean, stem originally from this desire for Love. In this way, we can truly begin to love our neighbors as ourselves, because we will realize once and for all that our neighbors ARE ourselves. We all spring from, live in and love as aspects of this One Grand Being we call God~Love~Source. This realization opens the doorway for even greater depths of service to emerge through us as gateways and portalways of this divine love. Divine self interest takes on a whole new meaning.

Do not be surprised if your heart swells with more love than you can handle. Allow tears to flow, joy to spread and understanding to seep in like never before as you practice such miraculous acts of healing as recognizing the One in the Many.

PRECEPT 3:
YOU WILL BECOME HARMLESS AS YOU MELT INTO A LIFE BASED UPON ONE AND TWO

"Do No Harm"
"Thou shall not kill"
"The meek shall inherit the earth"
"You must be as a little child to enter the kingdom"

We can witness now how and why one would become harmless when one practices loving God and loving others as Oneself. The pure love that we are at the core is not capable of causing harm. This love recognizes Itself in everyone and everything, and in it's healed state only desires to be, spread and know that love.

Keep in mind that this love is not devoid of humor. This love in fact is extremely playful, loving and child like, allowing all, witnessing all, and telling the truth. Mirthful joy and playfulness are not at all foreign but are a hallmark of this state of being. Life is fun! The religiosity, pain and suffering of our former age have made of everything, even the most sublime spiritual teachings, a torment for the soul. Now, we are reopening once again on a massive scale to the realization that life is about play, life is a play and we get to do just that.

Living from a place of Love's Eternal Embrace, witnessing God in all around you, leads you to a beautiful space of being where your only desire is for the expansion of this love. Where will love guide you next? What would love say or do next? How would love experience the most joy, fun and delight here and now?

We have this love at our beck and call. We can invite it to come play with us, as us and through us in all aspects of life. As we do so any places where we are still holding tight seriousness can begin to melt away. Any places within us where we still wish to harm, punish or chastise ourselves in any way can dissolve once and for all. Where we have habits we know are harming our bodies and keeping us from expressing our true gifts, the divine eternal Parent within us can have a new tone of voice—it can share the truth about what this habit is doing, and share how loved we are, so that we can be lovingly scolded without reproach and guided onto a path of better choices because we ourselves have chosen this new path and desire support on it.

We will eventually cease being able to harm ourselves in any way, with food, or unhealthy, unvibrant relations, with any substances or any activities that are not in alignment with our highest good. Our inner vibrational barometer will always steer us in the right direction as we seek love, see love, feel love and share love.

We can learn to be gentle with ourselves and others as we move through the final stages of our healing journey into an ability to express and live more light and love. Remember — the results of past actions called karma have accumulated through eons in our genetic lineages and in our past lives, so we must learn to be compassionate with ourselves and others, and grateful for everything that arises in life, knowing that it is simply the out-picturing of those past actions, words, thoughts and feelings which we are now experiencing. "Thank you for this release!"

"Thank you for liberating all beings!" "Thank you for this clearing!" For as we resist not what is upon us, we become more powerful to do our good work.

Nothing can resist a truly nonresistant being.
~Lao Tse

Remember Jesus said, turn the other cheek. This is because what comes upon you is probably yours energetically, returning to you like a boomerang. "Thank You God" is the quick path to enlightenment. "What I have sowed so have I now reaped and let it be done." Now we can truly understand what was meant by this teaching, and we can embrace the reality that to push against these boomerangs as they return to us is only to send them back into the ethers from which they will surely return to us again.

We catch the boomerang, give thanks for its return and put it down, giving it back to God, back to Love, to be transmuted and cleared once and for all by 'turning the other cheek,' giving thanks, and forgiving all involved. To do anything else is to continue spinning upon the wheels of karma indefinitely.

Eventually, by understanding the application of Universal principle, we will learn. Since we have also come into this world forgetting our past lives and largely unaware of the energetic inheritances of our genetic lineages, these boomerangs can feel like insults and smacks to the face which to be rectified need to be smacked back at.

So once again compassion for Self and Other as we work through these last remnants of karmic returns is of paramount usefulness. This is why we focus on Love even when chaos appears to be real in our lives. "Thank you God. Thank you for this release. Thank you for this completion." One grave misunderstanding is that God set things up this way to punish us.

Nothing could be further from the truth.

The Universal Principles of Life have been generated as a Divine Gift. Through them we can grow and learn at our own pace. In cooperation with them we can set ourselves and others free. They offer a self reflective, self monitoring set of tools through which we can clearly see the results of our own actions and choices.

If you were the supreme being and decided to extend yourself into form through the expression as countless beings masquerading as individuals, would you not give yourself the gift of free will?

And would you also not in your wisdom, give yourself a self-management and course correcting tool so that in the ensuing forgetfulness as you dropped your consciousness down into creation, you would have a context and a reality check with which to guide yourself back home to your former Unity when the time was ripe? Let's consider it from this perspective for a moment, and we can see how the all allowing nature of God as One Being in Many has simply cherished each aspect of Itself so much that it has created a format with which to center Itself in it's experiential adventure.

When we begin to identify with the grander Self from this perspective, Universal Justice can seen as already existent, it Just Is. From this place we can see why forgiveness is grand. For we are only forgiving ourselves. We are only setting ourselves free as we release and pardon other aspects of ourselves which have also been on this top secret free will adventure.

Now mercy and grace are aware that the suffering of beings who believe themselves to be separate, who have gotten so caught up in the game that they now do not remember their Oneness with Creator, is very, very great indeed. These experiences are real and not to be belittled or diminished. This is why Universal Principle also set up the Cycles of Ages so that certain aspects of Itself would emerge into density first, second, third and so on, so that on the return ride home, the aspects which went first would figure all of this out and be available to assist the next round of beings as they begin to awaken from the dream of separation. In this planetary experience, the acts of mercilessness and harm contrary from our Original Nature of Oneness and Love have been immense. Certain aspects of this One being made a decision to take the separation to the hilt of where it could go.

Whether in retrospect this was or was not a wise decision is open for debate. However, now the grand consensus is that the Game is over! Let the healing and reawakening begin.

- Is there only God (Goodness, Love), or not?
- If there is only God (Goodness, Love), all is ***ultimately*** well.
- Rest upon this knowing.
- Rest upon the Lord (The Law)
- Be At One, Be At-Oned.
- Be redeemed, sanctified and salvaged.

Chireya's Love Note: *Accepting All That Is As It Is and "Turning the Other Cheek" does NOT mean we need to stay in unbalanced, harmful or disrespectful situations. It simply means, we acknowledge that whatever the reflection, we somehow attracted it, knowingly or unknowingly. There is no need to stay and "suffer more" as there is no room for guilt in the truth of the love that we are. Tune in and trust your inner guidance, and seek out insight from loving,* *licensed professionals in any circumstance where you are experiencing someone harming you in any way and know that all is well as you choose to love yourself enough to change circumstances if necessary.*

We can see and understand these teachings which have been so twisted in a new light now. Redemption, Salvation, Sanctification, Atonement.

"We" are the various embodiments of Our Self saving ourselves from our own chosen experiential adventure in form, in our own time and in our own way. Rest upon this knowing. Just as your turn is emerging to be helped, so is your turn emerging to help others, of your own free choosing, in your own time, and in your own way. For truly, you and your brothers and sisters are One.

AN ALTERNATIVE VIEW OF A SECOND COMING

I do not want them to worship me this time.
Therefore I must hide myself in many places,
and simply shine, shine, shine.

In our discussions in this material we have come to see a history of humanity based on fear in which false histories have been in place and in which idle/idol worship has also had a vast grip on the consciousness of the people.[4]

If you were a Christ-like being, a Jesus, Buddha or advanced race of beings here to assist humanity lovingly and through free will choices in its process of awakening, here because there has been a 'vibrational request' by a sleeping humanity calling out to God for help in its torment of separation, how would you enact the next phase unfoldment of an authentic spiritual assistance and

---

[4] *Chireya's Note: Idol worship in this sense, refers to the fact that human beings have worshipped beings as God, instead of cultivating the direct Source connection with "God Within" that is their birthright and heritage.*

teaching in ways that would actually help rather than hinder humanity in its progress?

You would surely not wish to cause further separation through any action. You would surely do your best to avoid being made into an idol or a God to be falsely worshipped or put on a pedestal, and you would surely wish for humankind to see itself as equal to you, as siblings in the family of the One before revealing your face unto them again.

You would surely wish to avoid causing any further nonaligned religiosity or rote following of rules based on fear, and you would surely wish to do your best to help people reconnect with their own direct Source Connection so that they can come to know themselves as One with that Almighty Power behind all things.

The complete and total liberation from fear, servitude, falsehood and lies would surely be that which you would desire for your precious cosmic siblings in their wake up process. And so you would hide yourself. You would cloak yourself. You would show up in so many different places so that no one could grasp onto your personality as The One and Only. You would remain humble, simple and unadorned of any sort of grandiosity. You would love, love, and love some more. You might even be so wise and so bold as to hide your own identity from Yourself so that you might not be tempted to become the Exalted One again and have false pretenses played up around you, in your own ego personality structure or in that of others.

We are smiling now, along with you. Yes, it's true.

You would seek not for fame, glory or riches unless they came to you as a natural part of your role in the grand Mystery Play of the Awakening ~ the Revelation of the truth behind our history and our true nature. You would have learned through a deep dedication to remain non-attached to material wealth even while enjoying it, to understand it as a beautiful part of the ebb and flow of the creative impulse rather than a necessary stature upon which to base your approval or disapproval of yourself.

And you would be willing to undergo many challenges personally in order to be able to show up collectively as the Cosmic Alarm Clock is sounded and your earth siblings began to wake up. You would be living in the flow, on the precipice, in trust to whatever degree you had become able during any given preparatory incarnation. Even if you had bitten off more than you could chew and had dived into very dense, fear based family lineages and life experiences in an effort to heal the darkness, leaving you feeling fragmented, less than whole and somewhat unsure of yourself, you would still know deep inside to begin the work of personal healing and salvation that would allow you to have even more compassion for the human condition so that you could, at the right moment, serve in earnest in truly meaningful ways.

And you would have become completely willing to go through this knowing it would ultimately result in the desired outcome and that you are at your essence always At One with the one regardless of appearances or life experiences. You would have a deep inner knowing that you could return to Wholeness through your own efforts with the help of your team members over time.

And so, we find ourselves here, at this moment of grand awakening upon our beautiful planet earth. We find that we are finding each other — "other ones of ourselves" — who took the plunge, reminiscent of the Bodhisattva[5] promise to save all sentient beings. Then the work would begin in earnest, with joy, thanksgiving, hope and a whole lotta love.

You are the Second Coming. We are the Second Coming. The pure divine love, called by some the Christ Consciousness is available, now, on this planet, to all who seek it. There is not only one savior, for we shall all save ourselves and lift up a

---

[5] See Glossary for explanation of Bodhisattva

hand in service to assist one another in the restoration of our consciousness back into Pure Love.

Simply by living a life based on love and authentic, universal spiritual principles, and by continually working on clearing out the programming in your own consciousness, you are the Christed One here as a shining example to bring in a new day and live a new way with vast numbers of your brothers and sisters who are at one with you in this divine mission.

The hundredth monkey theory prevails as each of us work upon ourselves and shine our light. Truly this light manifests as change and awakening in the consciousness of the masses of humanity. Truly we can live the principle that the One is in the many and the many are in the One. Truly we can bear witness to the awakening of the "Grand I Whole" in the "I Am" of the Lord – God, the power of Love, and the "I" of each one of us. We shall more and more experience joy beyond measure as we realize the prophecies are being fulfilled and we are awakening together.

LIVING IN DIVINE PRINCIPLE

THE 5 DIVINE PRINCIPLES

- ETERNAL LOVE
- JUSTICE "JUST IS"
- NON-ATTACHMENT = FLOW
- RESONANT ATTRACTION
- ONENESS

This Five Pointed Star shows that these Principles are the key components for the Life of Humankind, and that they are all related and connected under One Universal Law, the Law of Love.

So where are we now and where are we going? We find ourselves on a lovely planet on the brink of so many disasters with an awakening sequence in place and at various stages of this awakening process, individually and collectively.

Each of us who are embodied here have opportunities every day to choose love instead of fear thereby further allowing the presence and power of love to penetrate the energetic matrix of this planet.

What are some of the key tools which will assist us and our cosmic and earthly siblings during this process? What are the ways and means by which we can incorporate, i.e., bring into the body these principles and live them fully, thus landing the new patterns birthed of love into our own lives and into the collective consciousness?

We say to you these ways are endless and many, and as you further attune to the love that you are, you will discover and create expanded ways and means to these ends.

In these materials, we wish to offer you some ideas to play with, not as rules but as gemstones to simply have about you or to leverage as tools.

These ways are in correspondence with the Light Codes of Ascension as conducted by the Masters of the Inner Planes who have gone before you in their own process of awakening on various planets at other times and in various dimensions.

These are sanctioned tools for your toolbox brought to you from, as and with Divine Love for your enjoyment, enlightenment, upliftment and expansion. If you feel any fear or discomfort associated with any of these principles, you can bet that there is a personality-based rule structure from a past religious or worldly experience associated with it that it would be helpful to clear out of your field. So as you read through this material, notice if you feel any fear, resistance, worry, hardness, judgment, or worry.

From within the heart of God and the Divine Mind, each of these principles act in synergy as One. It is challenging to explain this reality — to indicate it. The spiritual teachers and masters who have attained these states of awareness and realization, have done their best over the centuries to share insight from within this state of mind-heart-being to help the collective get closer and closer to the direct experience of it. From our vantage point, you can discern an authentic teaching if it has your direct realization of your Oneness with God and All That Is as its foundational goal.

Anywhere that you have a set of principles rules or guidance that is attempting to make you wrong in any way, attempting to make you feel bad, or feel as though you must suffer in order to grow, you know that this teaching is still muddied with separation thinking. Not to worry though; simply leverage your own Divine Intuition to sort the wheat from the chaff and pick out the goods which will serve you. Remember to leverage your consciousness of pure divine love in forgiveness of any and all whom you encounter who are still entrenched in ego dominated ways, and send them a quiet inner blessing for their journey home. Practice makes perfect! As we don our cap of awareness in our daily lives, we will have endless opportunities to practice, grow and learn, for the power of love is surely with us and has our great good in mind at all times.

We offer these principles listed below with a caveat: cling not unto these means and ways. Continue in the flow and always remember: ceremony, ritual, and acts of healing are a means to an end, they are not the end unto themselves. Therefore, be bold in your allowing, and be bold in your letting go. When a tool no longer serves you, when it has completed its mission, release it! Let go! Give it away! The next person shall truly find it useful on their path as you are guided to share, release and give away what has served its purpose for you.

Make not of them any stamped process that others must follow in order to aspire. Simply follow your own true inner guidance, and do share as you are guided, with the simple, loving non-attachment and trust that each being will be guided on their unique path in their perfect way by the One Source that loves and has Its life as us all.

The Five Divine Principles

PRINCIPLE 1:
ETERNAL UNCONDITIONAL LOVE

True unconditional love comes from deep wisdom and understanding. If we realize there is One Being behind all of Life, and that all Result has a Cause, then we can begin to embrace Eternal Unconditional Love. This is a process. It's okay that it is a process. Feel unconditional love for yourself to the greatest degree possible as this process unfolds.

Fear, money, pride and personality glorification all often masquerade as God. This tendency can be seen in ALL religions if one digs deep enough. Many Beings have masqueraded as God, setting forth rules and directives which seek to punish and control.

Disallow this from happening by allowing love to take precedence over all illusion as best you can every day. If we can frame our understanding of deeply imbedded words such as, "Thou shalt have no other God before Me" into meaningful and helpful potentials, we will allow "Me" in this instance to indicate for us the One True Source of All Life in which we each have our endless eternal Being.

In other words, an ETERNAL LOVE without conditions is One Principle which we would wish to cling to. Trust this Source within YOU to guide you. Trust yourself to follow this guidance.

How can we best grasp this Principle of Eternal Unconditional Love from within a world where the worship of the individuated personality reigns? If we can see that everyone who has ever been born was "breathed to life" by this One Spark, this "essence" of Life Itself, then we can see that truly, there is One Being operating behind the masks and masquerades of all.

Each person has different levels of conditioning, cultural belief, deeply ingrained patterns and habits and daily thoughts which allow or disallow the recognition of this One Life inside all of us, to varying degrees. This One Pointed Focus upon Eternal Unconditional Love therefore includes the AWARENESS that not all beings are AWARE of the reasoning behind Eternal Unconditional Love. Deep wisdom comes from fully embracing this realization. Compassion is the Child of our embrace with Wisdom.

Even so—even though many if not most people are not aware and may or may not become aware of this Oneness, WE are aware. Therefore in our wisdom, we can learn to live from this understanding even when others do not. This takes courage, boldness and a willingness to "live our edge." We will become better at finding the most appropriate words and actions for every situation as we embrace the Principle of Eternal Unconditional Love.

At times this Principle may require us to be Unconditionally Loving towards our own lack of Unconditional Love. We may become aware of tight spots and deep lines of engrained thought from which it is hard to extract ourselves. We may also become aware of aspects of our personality or behavior we wish were different. If we can extend this Eternal Unconditional Love to ourselves in these moments, then it becomes easier and easier to extend them to others in their pain, suffering or acting out. In this manner, the process of liberation begins.

PRINCIPLE 2:
FLOW, NON-ATTACHMENT

Release all attachments. Simplify.

The principle of non-attachment is one that has often been misunderstood. Many practitioners confuse this with an over-mentalization of life and a self-extraction from the heart centered realities of love and joy on the earth plane.

The non-attachment we are speaking of is neither austere nor painful. It does not require you to suffer in any way. It does not require you to feel superior or inferior to any other being. In fact, it is a natural consequence of practicing the first principle.

You will notice increasingly that you are naturally unattached to outcome as you live more and more in the Principle of One Pointedness. From within the heart centered reality of God Realization, the word non-attachment feels awkward and does not do the experience justice. That is why we are choosing to call this principle The Principle of Flow. It is a more accurate reflection at this time of what is truly being indicated here.

Life is always changing, amorphously blossoming into new forms of becoming and releasing. To cling to ideas, experiences, people, places and things beyond their appropriateness in your life and living is to be attached.

There is no one set rule for everyone around how to determine when you are in the flow and when you are attached. It is for each one to tune in and to become aware of what it feels like when you are in the flow, and what it feels like when you are attached.

- Flow feels open, allowing, expansive, kind, possibly even joyful, giddy and liberating.

- Attachment feels constrictive, emotionally or mentally painful to varying degrees, tiring, and ultimately boring.

Often our cultural or genetic belief systems will insist on certain practices of attachment to various forms of reproach as punishment when violating the rules upon which they insist. This is why it is often difficult or challenging to 'go with the flow.' Your energy wants to move you, to change you, to play with you and allow you to play in life, however, your "context" as possibly reflected in your community, wishes to constrain you so as to keep up the illusion of its own safety and permanence based on your acting a certain way.

Without such constrictions and belief systems, spiritual growth would occur much more quickly as more flow would be allowed. We are witnessing as an increasing number of beings are allowing themselves to move more and more fully into the divine stream of the flow of life. Remember too, there is a distinction between being in the flow and being spacey, ungrounded, irresponsible or lazy. These attributes would be the flip side of the polarized duality between attachment and ungroundedness. True Flow transcends both polarities and emerges effortlessly from within a unified field consciousness.

Simplify Life

Another aspect of the Principle of Flow and non-attachment has to do with simplifying life. In the dualistic mind set, this would look like austerity and poverty versus greed and hoarding. True simplicity springs forth from the knowing that our basic needs of life are truly simple. Beautiful natural settings, fresh air, clean water, pure food, divine friendship, celebration, naturally made items that do no harm to our environment, rest, movement, increase of skill, play, opportunities to share and acts of creation are what people really desire and need at a core level.

EXERCISE: Align with Flow & Simplicity

1. We offer an idea which may help you in aligning with the true nature of simplicity and flow.
2. Close your eyes, breathe deeply, and relax.
3. Imagine yourself as whole perfect and complete. Imagine yourself as satisfied, happy and delighted with life.
4. Really feel this feeling at the deepest possible level.
5. Now notice what if any people, places, and things are around you when you are naturally in this state.
6. Notice what you require and desire to sustain you in that space of pure happiness, if anything.
7. Now imagine your current life and all of your belongings, relationships, and all the places you go to, the things you purchase and consume.
8. Notice how you feel as you go through the actions of your daily life which things, interactions, items you consume, and places cause you to sustain this feeling of expansive joy, and which ones cause you to contract.
9. Take some notes after this and seriously consider what might be good to release from your life at this time.
10. Whether you are in your prime flow state with lots of beautiful belongings or with a monk-like

streamlined existence, know that you can attune to the flow which works best for you. There is no right or wrong way. You will know which way or ways are right for you as you hone your inner senses more and more.
11. Become willing to release those things which are no longer serving you. This may not always seem like an easy task. Sometimes through our life experience we have come into ways of being which are "other than" aligned with our highest expression of joy in life. Once again we want to leverage that ability to love ourselves and have compassion for ourselves, knowing we are where we are because we are where we are, and there is no judgment.

PRINCIPLE 3:
NON-JUDGMENT & JUSTICE "JUST IS"

Refrain from judgment.

From our examination in this book, we can see that the wheels of karma have been spinning for eons causing endless repercussions for countless beings in all places.

No being is exempt from this law of cause and effect. We can say that true divine justice "Just Is" because from the larger perspective, all truly is in divine order.

Just because we cannot remember our past lives and do not know the entire history of the DNA lineages we are carrying does not mean that these imprints have no impact on our current life experience. To the contrary, they do indeed.

Now, as the grand Witness watches all that has transpired, there is a complete lack of judgment, only a witnessing, an accepting, an allowing. The created beings who are extensions of this one life are subject to the action of this principle and as they progress in their development, eventually learn to 'be like this One,' this Witness which observes and allows without judgment. This does not mean a created being will not be inspired to work to cease harmful practices. It means that as we go about our business of making the world a better place, we do so from an elevated understanding in which we realize the balancing acts that are unfolding all around us from many, many lifetimes and lineage-based experiences which perpetuate patterns of thought, action and feeling.

Do you remember the song from John Lennon, where he sings, "I'm just sitting here watchin' the wheels go round and round, I really love to watch them roll. No longer riding on the merry-go-round! I just had to let it go!"

John, an advanced spiritual aspirant, realized that the wheels of karma churn and churn and churn until a soul decides of its own accord and its own wisdom to hop off and begin a higher game.

We are at such a juncture collectively now as we are moving from the game of karmic payback to the game of resonant attraction. We reset the zero point and move off the wheel as we choose to respond with love instead of fear. Accepting all as it is from a place of wisdom and understanding, we no longer judge it as bad, wrong or evil. No longer judging, we release ourselves from bondage to that cycle of experience. Love has set us free.

PRINCIPLE 4: ONENESS

Be ever yielding. Answer challenge or divisiveness with kindness.

Who are you again? Oh, right. The One, an aspect of the One Light that Is. The eternal, loving Source connected to, through, as and by all things. From this perspective, when we are 'in the way' with another aspect of ourselves, we practice being 'ever-yielding.' This ever yielding nature does not mean to be subjugated or dominated. It simply means to be respectful of those around you as other aspects of the One. To yield the right of way when you approach another at the same time-space point, to yield to another sharing first and deeply listening, to yield to love when the initial impulse is to come from a fear based reaction, are all very good and simple practices which can help remind us continually of our cosmic connection with all things and which can also assist us in maintaining that desired humility which keeps our ego personalities from running the show.

What about when someone is upset or angry with you? What if they are projecting on you? The Principle of Oneness can help you here as well. Sometimes it may anger people who are stuck in an ego drama or projection even more if you act kindly toward them when they are being unkind to you. At other times, an act of kindness in the face of someone's anger may help to soothe them. Either way, it is ultimately the highest response which will bear the greatest fruit. (See the section "Technique for Overcoming Projection When Experiencing An Emotional Charge" in Chapter 5 for assistance with this.)

A spiritual misperception in this territory might lead a being to give in to harsh treatment by others and to stay where that treatment exists. We are truly not suggesting this by any means. Quite to the contrary, when we really 'get' this principle of Oneness and Yielding, we open the doorway to our own freedom from such unpleasant energies. By "not reacting" to the negative energies of others, we begin to liberate ourselves energetically from such situations. Coupling this with the technique of overcoming emotional charges in ourselves, with an understanding of our own "responsibility" in drawing circumstances to ourselves, allows us to wind our way out into higher vibrations and situations.

It is good to allow yourself to FLOW out of destructive interactions into productive, harmonious situations. If it feels difficult or impossible to extract yourself from such a situation, it is likely there are karmic energies or seeds being worked out. In that case, the art of yielding will serve you well as you 'bow out' of arguments gracefully and choose to go within to work out the emotional charge you may be experiencing instead of projecting it back on the other. In this way little by little, you will be extracting yourself from the situation.

As the saying goes, the negative energies will either depart or transform as those energies are completed within ourselves. Acts of love, kindness, gratitude, celebration and forgiveness all cause these energies to transform more quickly than they otherwise would, so we can leverage this knowledge by intentionally focusing upon these high vibrational thought forms through any negative experiences.

A simple switch of our attention over to something beautiful can sometimes be enough to change an entire life's course when deep negativity has reared its head. To shift one's awareness WITH a deep and respectful awareness of the energies at hand and a total focus is a very powerful act of ending old patterns and beginning new, positive ones.

Our ability to yield and to refocus our consciousness are direct attributes of our awareness of our Oneness. Because we are connected in our consciousness to the greater I AM Whole Being that We Are as One, this larger Being understands everything about all the situations at hand. It has 'got you covered,' so to speak. So when you are in an encounter with another being, there is NOTHING this larger fullest aspect of Who we are does not know about either of you, all your past life times, and all of your ancestral genetic lineage inheritances.

Therefore, inviting in the awareness of this Oneness gives you vibrational access not only to the historical data but also to the Source's best method of clearing and healing the energies and cords between this other child of God with whom you are in the way. You may or may not require to know all of this historical data tacitly. It may be enough to simply request that all negative energies and cords and histories between and among you both (or among you all) and your genetic lineages be cleaned and cleared now for the highest good of all. This prayer request can be made non-verbally and even energetically simply by your base-level intention for creating harmony and healing wherever you go. It can also be helpful to speak this prayer intention out loud, for instance:

Divine One, God, Love, please help me to forgive,
release and love unconditionally
_____ [name of person].

Please help _____ [name of person]
to forgive, release and love me
unconditionally. Thank you God.

Deeply listening to the other in distress is one of the most important gifts we can give to us and them. Trust yourself to know when the energies are crossing the line into abusiveness toward you, and distinguish when you can still hold the space of love necessary to restore the harmony between you. And do not hesitate when called to invite the assistance of other practitioners of Light and Love when remediation is desired between you and another. Sometimes that third witness space holder, if advanced enough, can really help to deeply listen to the entire story and invite in the larger perspective so that a feeling of unity and Oneness can be restored.

PRINCIPLE 5:
RESONANT ATTRACTION

- Become a resonant attractor by working in harmony with the laws of cause and effect.
- Celebrate life and live from love.
- In doing so you can know without a shadow of a doubt that you are attracting more and more goodness into your life and into the life stream of the planetary sphere.

As we become increasingly aware that our thoughts, words, feelings and actions bring forth experiences into our lives, we have more incentive to focalize our thoughts, words, feelings and actions towards those results of our choosing. In this way, we begin to attain toward Mastery of Life.

This Mastery allows us to be the divine choosers we are meant to be.

In the simplest of ways, by radiating and expanding love, harmony and gratitude, only that vibration will return to us. If something else returns to us, we simply remember that that something must be ours from a previous incarnation or from the coding within our genetic lineages. We call upon forgiveness of ourselves and all others involved and continue to choose love instead of fear. In that way, the karmic cycle is completed and we come into greater and greater resonance with the forces of Love which seek to nurture and please us. And if we choose, we can magnify these feelings, thoughts, actions and words towards very specific aims of our own choosing.

For now, let's simply rest in the knowing that as you invite your Source Creator, God, Love into the conversation along with the consciousness of your Mother Planet, all of nature, and your beautiful light being Guides, you will receive input, inspiration and guidance which will allow your manifestations to be of the highest order of divine goodness for you.

Living In Resonance equates to living in harmony. You call upon and manifest into your life those people, places, things, consumables and scenarios which truly exist in resonant harmony with your greater good and therefore the greater good of the Whole.

CLOSING MESSAGE

There is only one being, only one power, only one presence. The mystery of this fact is being revealed to millions of people more and more each day.

The fact of our Oneness pre-exists the experience of our separation. Our Oneness has not died or faded away during the times of separation, it has merely been hidden from us, elusive and bold, ever present yet playing hide and seek, dressed in various strange garments.

Never has there been a time when this power of Love has not been with us, and never will there be such a time.

The out-picturing of the illusory game of pain, blame, shame, suffering, loss, grief, death, hardship, destruction, hate, fear, harming, envy, greed, control and manipulation has been a very real experience causing real repercussions in our consciousness, on our planet and in our bodies.

As we begin in full this awakening sequence, it is time to crystallize the vibrations of the pure divine love that we are, to coalesce our particles so to speak, into very high, strong, resonant energy fields which will support us and our loved ones and our communities in holding these love frequencies as powerfully as possible.

The power of love is not to be underestimated. For even as the shift hits the fan more and more, we seek to offer you assistance in learning to hold this power of love, to project it, to use it and to share it to protect yourselves, to bless your communities and to build the new systems, structures and way of being that will support countless generations to come in ever advancing, more and more harmonious ways of living on this beautiful planet.

We beseech you to reside ever more fully in this power and presence of love. Truly this love creates the resonant force field which will make the shift times as graceful as possible for you and your loved ones. Do not hesitate for a second to call upon the power of Love in times of need, strife or struggle. As you and your family and friends move through various layers of the old energies surfacing for clearing, there will likely be many instances of opportunity for you to practice holding this beautiful and divine field of true, inspired love. Simply holding this field of love above, below and all around about you and the people you are with will begin to soften any rough edges during confrontations or moments of sadness and love. Leveraging the pure power of unconditional love for all people, places, circumstances and things will assist you in personally aspiring to that greatness of consciousness which you know is yours, in lasting ways.

Remember that any and all action of harming, blame, hate, or judgment comes from within this core wound. There is a space of love that can heal even the deepest wounds and restore peace even in the midst of the greatest tragedies. Have compassion for yourself and your human family as you ride through these times. Be the harbinger of the true love you were born to be. Leverage the power of spirit to bring a smile to all situations and embrace all sadness with a deep hug of compassionate forgiveness.

Your brothers and sisters need you to be the great rebalancing energies that see past the dismantling energies into each of their capacity for joy and light and goodness. You can hold a powerful space for transmutation simply by inviting in the One All Seeing Eye, the I AM that We Are into any conversation. Do not be surprised if increasingly you find yourself with opportunities to witness and shine love upon individuals with differing views or even in conflict. When we can see from the perspective of the very long history of our separation experience how so much woundedness has built upon layers of previous wounds all based on a feeling of being separated from love, we can begin to have compassion even for those we call criminals and those who have harmed others. From the largest perspective, we can bring in a space of love wherever there is conflict and judgment to help all see and feel that they need not be judged, they need not judge. We don't do this by telling them they are wrong. We do this by witnessing what is trying to be expressed and expressing it back clearly to assist people in the cessation of projection.

The habit of projection is the greatest cause of conflict. Deeply buried or surface level traumas get outpictured from the telescope of our own minds and projected onto the movie screen of the others that show up in our lives. When people are unaware of this function of reality, the tendency is to blame, shame, expect and project anger. Ultimately, through an experience of 'not' being judged, people can begin to heal and to see that our collective decision to descend into density and to experience this dimension in these ways with free will has led to suffering.

Not a single one of us has been exempt from this suffering. Love can see each point of view as valid simultaneously and can hold it all in a cauldron of deep witnessing and allowing. This powerful embrace makes people feel they are being seen and heard. Since being denied, ignored and even stomped out has been a very common experience, this simple act of seeing and hearing a person's point of view, especially if others are angry with them, is immensely healing.

To hold this role as space holder for humanity is to come to be at one with the deepest levels of humility. For truly an opinionated ego who feels it and only it knows the true way will not have the power to sustain the energies at hand. The humility which comes from having been re-birthed through a cauldron of transmuting fire within one's own inner temple and one's own life experience is the gift of grace which will indeed allow you to serve at the highest level and to see with the clearest eyes. God's servants do not seek to further divide humanity. They seek to restore love, unity, harmony and peace between all beings who are willing to experience this peace. You are one of these beings. Feel into this deeply and embrace your true calling with great joy and pleasure, for you have earned it.

The memory banks which store your remembrance of your divine heritage are still within you. You can never lose them. Through countless eons of experience you have traveled as on a grand voyage. Through countless more eons you will return with your brothers and sisters to the One Light Home within the primal sound and being of God as God. Fear not the journey, for you will discover as you progress more and more joy, more and more light, more and more exuberance. You will discover that all your painstaking work to improve yourself, awaken yourself and shine your light have, do and will bear the delicious and sumptuous fruit of freedom for you and others.

Keep a smile on your face and remember to stoke the fires of radiant love within your heart and you will always be guided and protected. Do not deny yourself when issues or suffering emerges for yourself or others. Simply allow, love and caress these energies into total release, knowing that all is well even when it appears otherwise. Seek the divine insight, seek the wisdom, and release any blame or judgment for the situation so that you can see clearly with God's eyes for a moment as you witness the grand unfolding and unfurling of twisted old sails.

The greatest misperception of all has been to think that Prime Creator, God, our Source, is punishing us for wrongdoing. We are well informed to correct this thinking-feeling-belief on all levels of our consciousness, as the truth is, everything that has been brought into the experience of everyone has been wrought by their own hands, one way or another, knowingly or unknowingly. Do not make the mistake of judging others for their karmic deliveries, or chastising them when they have manifested something other than desired. This we could call spiritual bigotry and is quite unbecoming to an enlightened soul. Of course when you witness your brothers and sisters doing this, simply rest in the knowing that they will learn and grow beyond such behaviors. If you are called to lovingly correct this with words and feelings that can be received by all without resistance, we encourage this. Follow and trust always the guidance of your own heart and know that sometimes the silent witness of all is the most potent transformational cauldron available to us.

This is an amazing collective journey, one that truly boggles the mind. What is consciousness? How did all this come about? Why did this process get started, and how is it perpetuated? These and other mysteries are ours to discover as we grow and learn on the path. Truly we can see ourselves as taking part in the greatest reality show ever created. To acknowledge the humor of it all is powerful indeed. Joy, humor, simplicity and love are the hallmarks of this great awakening, of enlightenment.

We wish you all goodness on your continued journey. Please know, we are in service to the One, and are here with you and for you, always.

~ Star Elders of the Council of Human Enlightenment
~ Star Elders of the Council of Mu

CHIREYA'S TIPS FOR RECALIBRATING YOUR LIFE

COMPREHENDING COMPOUNDING MOMENTUM & GETTING OUT OF THE TRAP

I tuned in with Source, First Mother and First Father to co-create a basic "cheat sheet" to help us more quickly comprehend the interrelated intricacies of the teachings. Truly it is all quite simple! It is a different way of seeing the world and how it works, which is why things like "cheat sheets" can be useful, as we recalibrate our thought processes back to a greater spiritual comprehension of the "base software platform of reality."

The Universe has been set up on a "what you do, you get back" software platform. There has been so much "doing and getting back" for so long that people got confused and forgot how everything works. This is what we call "compounding momentum." The energetic results of this compounding momentum show up as real life experience. Sometimes, this experience is not pleasant.

People forget that they in this life, their past lives, or their relatives in their ancestral lineage set these energetic results into motion, somewhere along the line.

This forgetfulness causes confusion, because people don't comprehend the "why" of the reflection coming to them in their experience, especially if it's not fun.

This confusion can lead to pain, despair, suffering, and all manner of grief. Questions like "Why me?" and "What did I do to deserve this?" may emerge.

These questions filtered through the Cosmic Consciousness of a human being typically cause a chain reaction of self-made beliefs to be set into place such as, "Life is not fair," "I must be unworthy," "It's someone else's fault," "God must not love me," etcetera, ad infinitum.

Since people are still Creators attributed with all the creational forces of Source, regardless of whether they remember this or not, the plot thickens by the Source energy flowing through these non-aligned, skewed, false beliefs and projections, causing EVEN MORE unwanted stuff to flow in.

Because beliefs have been formed in an unaware attempt to make sense of it all, people then think it's okay to send destructive thoughts and feelings towards others, who must be "to blame" for all this crazy stuff happening to them.

And of course, people blame and think destructive thoughts generating destructive feelings towards themselves as well.

However, they forgot that this means these thoughts and energies will eventually compound and return to their maker.

At this point, the compounding momentum just keeps compounding. It's as if your ancestors put $10,000 into a bank account before you were born, and now it's worth $10,000,000,000,000. While much of this overactive bank account may contain divine gifts of spirit and flesh, it may also contain a lot of hoo ha and cosmic repercussions that we just hadn't bargained for from our conscious perspective!

While perhaps being a little enervating, this comprehension and analogy also makes it a little easier to understand why we are "where we are at" in the grand scheme of things.

"Oh, what to do?" may be the next question you ask. (Wink.)

In other words, how do we resolve this compounding spiraling energetic "situation" and reemerge in new spirals of Divine Deliberate Co-Creation on purpose, with our own original divine Blueprint as the base pattern for our creations? We invite in Source, Divine Mother, Divine Father and the spirit of Mercy and Grace to assist us, and attune, align, dissolve and design! This is called Recalibration. (See Appendix I. Resources for more information on the Recalibration Process™.)

The Master Key To Liberation

As Divine Mother says, "Unconditionally loving all that is as it is, is the Master Key to liberation. Your Divine Essence knows this and has been attempting to help you comprehend the why's and wherefores of this Eternal Love, forgiveness, non-attachment and self-acceptance. We cannot liberate ourselves or others through judgment. What is, IS. This is the Great IS IS of cosmic co-creation. To deny it, make it wrong, push against it, judge or hate 'what is' only causes MORE OF THE SAME. It is time my beloved Children, that you awaken from your foolish ways of self-absorption creating negative compounding results, and instead embrace the TRUTH OF YOU as Cosmic Co-creators. It is with all my love that I chastise you at this time, as I know you are ready for Truth."

Love Note from Chireya: *Remember, Source, God, Divine Mother, and Divine Father are already within us, as the Primary essence of our very own Being, from before the beginning of time and through the end of time. And, rule of thumb: whatever shows up, it's yours. Forgive it, thank it, bless it, and move on. Or if it's a yummy creation you're enjoying, congratulate yourself for attracting it and simply say, "More please!"*

First Mother and First Father sprang from Source as the Original Generating Energies of Creation. They through us fuel the e-motion (energy in motion) that manifests the phenomenal world. This is a mystery I will leave you to contemplate, and will be addressed further in the book series Codes of Union. In the meantime, please know that you can find and connect with First Mother, First Father, God, Source Love directly ~ Within You. Even as we remain the prodigal sons and daughters of God in our own minds and experience, or perhaps we still see ourselves as beggars at the Door of God, yet and still we can "know, sense, feel, accept, and be willing to accept the truth: "Ye are Gods." ~ Jesus the Christ

Action Steps for Recalibrating Your Life

From The Recalibration Process™ with Chireya

1. Take 100% responsibility for our lives, period. (Divine Father's Gift. Without taking up this Mantle of Truth, we stay victims forever. No thanks! With this gift, we get our power back.)

2. Recognize our 100% innocence, period. (Divine Mother's Gift. We did not "mean" to cause all

this trouble for ourselves when we started as baby spirits eons ago in our creational process.)

3. Sit in the Energies of Source, recognizing and embracing our 100% Divinity, Responsibility & Innocence (or fake it till you make it). Allow Source to simply wash over you, dissolving all of this, and inspiring you to your True Essence, True Energy, and True Life Path. The karmic samskaric residue[6] will eventually wash away due to the attenuation to the vibrations of Pure First Source, Prime Creator Energies. This is our foundation, our light, our beginning, and our end. This is "unconditional love," and love heals all things. Eternal, Effulgent, Overflowing and Abundant Grace, Mercy, Light, Love and Harmony flow from this Direct Source Connection, and will ALWAYS be available, from within your very own heart, soul, mind and spirit. Go there. Just do it. Your intention and free will choice to align with Source directly is more powerful than you think.

4. Do any clearing work that feels aligned with you, to resolve and dissolve away any of the

---

[6] See Appendix II: Glossary of Terms for Explanation of Karmic Samskaric Residue

overlays or energetic residue from past creations that were not conscious, that may be blocking the new vision. (See Appendix II: Resources for ideas.)

5. Retrieve and receive your aligned vision for your new life, in divine co-creation with Source within you (whatever you choose to call Source). There are many ways to do this, and you can create wonderful things to assist you in keeping your focus on these fabulous qualified, sanctioned visions! Vision boards, audio scripts, affirmations, energetic recalibrations, and aligning your vibrations to the positive feelings dial on a daily basis are just a few handy tools for this step. (For further ideas on how to accomplish step 4, see VisionSalon™ in Appendix II: Resources.)

6. Pay attention. Now that you've set all this in motion, things will start getting real interesting. Take action when the inspiration hits! Following the inspiration will lead you to actions that will help bring your visions to life.

Then, start the process all over again for anything you wish to create in your life! Truly, as big and large and expansive as all this seems, it's as simple as riding a bike. The truth is already within you!

You already ARE who you are. Your bigness and hugeness exceeds even your own wildest imagination. Yet you are also still the adorable, beloved "human" self having a human experience in 3D. What a trip! We are winding up the Grand Reunion of ourselves to Ourself. It is the greatest adventure available to us, and all signs indicate we are Ripe for the awakening. No one can do the steps of ascension for us, it's an inside job.

Remember, there were steps involved in learning how to ride a bike. There are steps to waking up to the truth of you. I know who you are.

You can do it.

Love,

Chireya

APPENDIX I: RESOURCES

CONNECTING WITH CHIREYA

For free audios, inspirational posts, online courses, events and private sessions including The Recalibration Process™, please visit Chireya on the web.
LovesWhisperings.com
Chireya.com

HELPFUL HEALING & CLEARING RESOURCES

Any kind of psycho-spiritual energetic healing will assist. Tune in and ask for guidance for the best practices for you. Here are a few that you may find useful:

- **The Recalibration Process™**
  Energetic Recalibration, Mental-Emotional-Spiritual Healing, Clearing, Vision Coaching & Life Design Mentoring with Chireya. See web links above.

- **Online Courses with Chireya**
  See web links above.

- **Free Star Elders Audio Recordings**
Recorded by Chireya, these are available for free. See AUDIOS link at Chireya.com.

- <u>Panacea Life School</u> is an online school based on the 13 Facets of Human Experience brought through by Chireya. This 13-month Course is truly life changing and life enhancing. Chireya is one of 5 originating teachers, including Founder Nathan Crane, with Cristina Smith, Darity Wesley and David Dibble.

- Ho'Opono'Pono ~ the practice of radical forgiveness from the Hawaiian Huna tradition. (There are many different types of practitioners. Do a google search and especially be sure to watch Dr. Hew Len's videos on youtube. In them, he explains what Ho'Opono'Pono truly is.)

- Soul Clearing (There are many different types of practitioners and modalities. Do a google search for soul clearing, access and clearing blockages.)

- EFT - Emotional Freedom Technique (There are many different types of practitioners. Do a google search. Chireya's dear friends Sonya Sophia,

Shafiya Eve and Jennifer Partridge are all reliable and helpful EFT practitioners.)

- Astrology, Human Design and other personality typing systems can help you in discovering some of the hidden blockages and patterns that you are living and course correct. Utilized these if and as you feel called, as a part of an overall self-awareness and recalibration process. Tune in and follow your intuition about which practitioners are best for you.

- Dream Healer - Dream Healer has a beautiful set of DVDs which can assist you in "seeing" the light work that can be done to cause physical healing to take place energetically. I highly recommend these dvd's for anyone seeking to become better and manifesting, creating and healing with light.

- 3 Magic Words Movie - I recommend the movie for those who wish to comprehend their divine nature. This is a film that shouldn't be missed by anyone at any spiritual level.

APPENDIX II. GLOSSARY

AFFIRMATIONS
Affirmations help us to say yes to those thoughts, feelings and actions we wish to full embody. It is good to speak them aloud, or record them and listen to them frequently to help shift states, bring in new mindsets and generally feel better.

AKASHIC RECORDS
The Akashic Records exist beyond all time and space and 'house' or contain all information, all data, all knowledge, all events, all experiences, all perceptions and perspectives and all past, present and future life timeline records for all beings on all dimensions. Certain people know how to access the Akashic Records to retrieve information that will be helpful to others for specific purposes of healing and aligning with their own innate nature and Divine Will.

BODHISATTVA
The Bodhisattva is one who has "vowed to save all beings," meaning they have advanced on the spiritual path through many lifetimes, and have decided they wish to be of service in the spiritual liberation of all beings throughout the cosmos who

have been stuck in the karmic-samskaric patterns, looping endlessly and unable to get free on their own. Bodhisattvas recognize that all beings are in fact aspects of themselves, and are therefore simply spiritual teachers dedicated to this grand unfoldment where eventually, all will remember and return to love.

CLEARING
The act of clearing helps us to release old patterns, energetics, thought forms, habits, mindsets and conditions which are outworn and dreary or causing us trouble in life. Clearing is a crucial part of the healing process. Clearing is done on all levels, physical, emotional, mental, spiritual, genetic, past-present-future life, and on all dimensions, in all concepts of time.

HEALING
At this time on planet earth, humankind is undergoing a great healing and clearing. We have lived through many incarnations of doubt, fear, worrying and suffering. We have a beautiful opportunity to awaken in the light of our True Nature, leveraging the assistance of our Creator, Source, and all levels of life which care about us and want us to aspire. We have many cheerleaders on many levels. So as we each open to the unique healing experiences we require for our own healing

and enlightenment, we assist the whole of humanity in awakening to its true nature, divine birthright and heritage as children of the Divine, whole, at one and in love with Life.

KARMIC SAMSKARIC RESIDUE
The energetic manifestations of past actions left as imprints on the subconscious and as rivulets of "tendency" in the neural pathways of the brain. Karma depicts the nature of the base software platform of reality, which is, that which goes out will come back to you. Samskaras are the rivulets or ruts in the brain also called neural pathways, which are a result of the karmic actions or tendencies, which compound themselves over time and become stronger, therefore harder to break. For example, someone whose parents smoked and then started smoking themselves, might have a really hard time stopping because of the depth of the "karmic samskaric residue" of these actions imprinted in the mind, body and emotions over time.

MANIFESTING
Our Source Creator endowed us with the attributes of the Creator. We have the powers of speech, action, thought, feeling and visualization to bring forth experiences into our lives. As we leverage these powers with a direct Source connection and a pure intent, we can help shift the lives of our

families, communities and ourselves for the better, with true joy!

MEDITATION

Meditation helps us go deep within to inner states of connection with the Divine Essence with which we are One. The key suggestion of the Star Elders is for us to meditate upon what it is our mind is doing — such that we can become aware of how we are creating a certain vibration with our thoughts. Simply becoming aware of our thoughts helps us to be able to redirect thought towards things we actually wish to manifest.

Since each thought is a seed, it is important to only nurture and water seeds that we want to grow.

PRAYERS

Prayers to God / Source / Life assist us in making that direct connection to our Creator. All of life springs from this Creative Source many call God. God the Mother, God the Father, the Spirit of Life, Holy Spirit… by whatever Name you choose, God is always with us. Prayers help us establish that knowing and that Divine Connection within. God can be found in religions yet is Universal and everywhere, bound by no person, place, idea or thing. Our connection to our Creator is pure, loving and always established in creating the Highest Good for ourselves, our community and our world.

PRECEPT
A precept is typically understood as a religious rule. In the Star Elders' use of this word, it is used two ways: 1. To indicate a piece of religious teaching that may have been twisted into a rule-based command that may or may not be based on your best interest. 2. In the section on the 3 Divine Precepts, the Star Elders are indicating a piece of instructional guidance with a foresight that is felt to be of high importance in the priorities of the teachings, towards the aim of further empowering the student.

PRINCIPLE
Principle indicates a fundamental, primary, or general law or truth from which others are derived. Principles are foundational to the overall comprehension of the teaching.

PROJECTION
Projection is the act of projecting one's own subconscious belief structures and patterns onto others without being aware that you are doing so. It is a natural and understandable tendency of people who have been through a separation experience. However, it is one of the main stumbling blocks to building community and healing relationships. There are many tools and skills available now to move through projection into a unified field consciousness which will allow true healing and

mutual understanding, growth, expansion and co-creation to occur.

RESONANCE
Resonance occurs when entrained thoughts and vibrations come into a matching harmony, generating energy, flow, cohesion, light and a loving awareness of oneness. We can generate resonance through heart-based practices in group settings for the purposes of alignment, attunement, and the creation of great efficiency and effectiveness.

YOUR FIELD
Your Field indicates the energetic matrix and aura of your personal being. We have many bodies, not just the physical body. We operate on mental, emotional, physical and ethereal levels and on various dimensions of consciousness. When a healer looks at you to 'see' what the blockages are or what your strengths are, they are looking at your Field. Healers and seers access this awareness through a direct connection with what we call the Unified Field.

UNIFIED FIELD (THE FIELD)
The Unified Field is the larger expanded energy and informational field which includes everyone, every planet, every galaxy and every thing in all of these simultaneously throughout all time and space. In

another context, the Unified Field can be used to indicate a strong resonant container energetically created by the participation of numerous individuals who come together for a common purpose.

VIBRATIONAL SIGNATURE
Your vibrational signature is the specific seed patterns or blueprints which make you unique between and among all created beings. Advanced beings can recognize one another tacitly through interaction with this vibrational signature. Our vibrational signature can get muddied or thwarted through experiences in a separation consciousness, and any act of healing largely resembles an act of recalibration to our original, unique signature.

CHIREYA

About The Author & Scribe

Creator of Anchor The Dream™, Chireya is an artist, writer, vision coach, life path mentor, seer, workshop facilitator, healing practitioner & speaker who assists individuals, organizations and communities by facilitating The Recalibration Process™.

Her books, sessions, workshops, audios and online courses assist people in manifesting their highest destiny path. A Scribe and Orator for Prime Creator / Source, First Mother, First Father, the Ancient Ones, Masters of the Light, Star Elders, and Mother Earth, Chireya enjoys helping people make real progress in the areas of their life's purpose, healing relationships & changing habits in ways that cultivate spiritual awakening, mind-mastery, heart awakening and nutritional upgrades.

As a student of the Law of Attraction, Chireya believes that, if we do have this power to create and manifest as Creators in our lives, we ought to apply ourselves to the study of this until we reach mastery. And, we ought to leverage these powers not only on behalf of our own good, (which we should do), but also we ought also to leverage them on behalf of all of humanity and all of nature. Last but not least, our responsibility is also to learn how to master and share these truths in collaboration with others, as truly, we are stepping into the age of collaboration at this very moment.

Thus, from this thought process, Chireya birthed the Anchor The Dream™ process of Visionary Theater, Music, Dance & Art for the purpose of "creating blueprints for earth life based on agendas of our own choosing." From the Anchor The Dream Experience, the body of work known as Collaborative Visioning & Visionary Stewardship has sprung.

At the heart of all her work is a deep desire to cultivate and serve the emerging genius and heart based soul awakening of individuals and groups around the world; for through this manifestation of healed and awakened beings, we will achieve beauty, grace and joy ~ heaven on earth, a golden age ~ which all the great prophecies have foreseen.

The Star Elders and Ancient Ones who birthed lineages of light and love to help us awaken to our mastery at this powerful time, are speaking to us through Chireya in a series of audio recordings, public appearances and writings including this book, to assist us in our collective shifting and awakening.

She helps groups accomplish the visioning work and inner healing work necessary to create collective resonance and experience higher order collaboration in which all the parts of the whole can dance together beautifully.

Chireya also provides advanced spiritual-emotional healing work to those who are drawn into her sphere, as a service towards the empowerment and awakening of individuals to fulfill their divine spiritual missions here on earth with great joy.

To contact the author, please visit
LovesWhisperings.com

www.ingramcontent.com/pod-product-compliance
Lightning Source LLC
LaVergne TN
LVHW051518070426
835507LV00023B/3171